TRAGEDY

TRAGEDY

Contradiction and Repression

Richard Kuhns

The University of Chicago Press | Chicago & London

RICHARD KUHNS is professor of philosophy at Columbia University. His previous books include *The House, the City, and the Judge: The Growth of Moral Awareness in the "Oresteia"* (1962) and *Psychoanalytic Theory of Art: A Philosophy of Art on Developmental Principles* (1983).

The University of Chicago Press, Chicago 60637
The University of Chicago Press, Ltd., London
© 1991 by The University of Chicago
All rights reserved. Published 1991
Printed in the United States of America
00 99 98 97 96 95 94 93 92 91   5 4 3 2 1

Library of Congress Cataloging-in-Publication Data

Kuhns, Richard Francis, 1924–
    Tragedy : contradiction and repression / Richard Kuhns.
        p.   cm.
    Includes bibliographical references and index.
    ISBN 0-226-45826-1
    1. Tragedy.   2. Psychoanalysis and literature.   I. Title.
PN1891.K84   1991
809.2'512—dc20   90-20279
                                                            CIP

⊗ The paper used in this publication meets the minimum requirements of the American National Standard for Information Sciences—Permanence of Paper for Printed Library Materials, ANSI Z39.48-1984.

To the memory of my mother and father
Helen Kuh Kuhns and Richard Francis Kuhns

It is ful fair a man to bere him evene,
For al day meeteth men at unset stevene.

Contents

Acknowledgments

"Why We Find Tragic Representations Pleasurable," which appears here as chapter 3, was presented in 1988 in a somewhat different form to Grand Rounds, psychiatric staff, Cornell Westchester Medical Center. In addition, the substance of two essays, "The Beautiful and the Sublime" and "The Strangeness of Justice: Reading *Michael Kohlhaas*," which appeared in *New Literary History* in 1982 and 1983 respectively, form parts of chapters 4 and 5 of this book. I am grateful to the sponsors and editors for permission to use these materials here.

It has been my good fortune to teach and study in a setting where I can go exploring with the companionship and help of friends in many disciplines. A stroll down Broadway, a climb to the top floor of Philosophy Hall typically produce fruitful encounters that complement the numerous formal opportunities for discussion that have informed my understanding. My thanks to all who have been, in ways often unknown to them, participants in this set of inquiries. I would like here to acknowledge the special contributions of a few.

I owe a debt to Helen Bacon, whose rare sensitivity to the imagery, language, and mythic aspects of Greek tragedy has enabled me to read the plays of Aeschylus with greater appreciation of their moral and poetic import than would otherwise have been possible. Eric Marcus, the psychoanalyst, with whom I have in recent years taught a seminar on the philosophy of art and culture, has been a constant source of stimulation and challenge in my exploration of psychoanalytic thinking; I have benefited enormously from commerce with his lively mind. Peter and Ruth Gay have helped with such a variety of criticisms, comments, and exploratory discussions over many years that I can only thank them for showing me how much can be done with psychoanalytic and historical interpretations of culture. From Peter Gay's vast and penetrating contribution to psychoanalytic theory and interpretation of cultural history, I mention here particularly his methodological analyses, which have brought a sophisticated understanding to the early efforts of what was originally termed "applied psychoanalysis." And from Ruth Gay I have gained an appreciation of creative historical research that preserves, in all its complexity, a sense of the past, while acutely realizing contemporary relevance. To Arthur Danto, colleague of many years in the arts and philosophy, who always finds the way through a difficult problem with ingenuity and imagination, my debt is too deep and many-sided to be put in a word of acknowledgment.

Others who have contributed to my thinking in special ways are Dieter Henrich, whose philosophical depth in both German and Anglo-American philosophy, as well as literature, has illuminated the affinities between philosophy and literature; André Green, whose brilliant analyses and interpretations of tragedy have opened my eyes to much of which I otherwise would have remained unaware; Theodore Reff, whose knowledge of and insight into modern painting have introduced me to subtle art-historical methods and interpretations; and Richard Wollheim and Leo Steinberg, whose thinking has been fundamental in bringing together conceptually the disciplines of philosophy, art history, and psychoanalytic theory.

I would like also to thank David Carrier for his discussion and criticism of the manuscript, as well as for inspiration from his remarkable way with philosophy and art history; and T. David Brent of The University of Chicago Press, for his care and thoughtful understanding through the process of publication.

Finally, I would like to make a special acknowledgment of the help and insight of Barbara Tovey and the late George Tovey, dear friends with whom I have journeyed through so many chapters of philosophical and literary discussion. "I think of the rock singing, and light making its own silence / At the edge of a ripening meadow, in early summer . . ."

Introduction

Tragic Experience and Tragic Vision, Old World and New

An apparent irony in the experience of tragedy has exercised a fascination down through the ages. Tragedy has been much admired and enjoyed as it unfolds in depictions of suffering, death, and the unexpected, if not undeserved, miseries imposed by fate; tragedy proves itself high entertainment as it reflects all that human wish would repel, erase, deny. Why do we remind ourselves of the saddest when we could have the happiest endings?

Philosophy has often looked askance at this state of affairs, yet philosophy and tragedy have maintained a puzzling symbiosis throughout the millennia—ever since Greek philosophy realized it had to take tragedy seriously, and tragedy, for its part, ventured deeply into philosophic thought. Philosophy thought *about* tragedy, sometimes rejecting its importunate advances with argument, sometimes retreating to its own claim of a deeper wisdom. As if in answer, tragedy went its own way, shedding its dark light and representing problems that philosophy hardly dared to touch. Withal, however, tragedy won more applause than philosophy could readily tolerate, so reprisals have been common, as between siblings raised together but with a mystery in their genealogies that never gets resolved.

Philosophy is an old broom that knows the corners and misses a good pile of the dust in the middle of the room, while new brooms designed to sweep clean often will not fit into the corners. So in the studies that follow I shall speak philosophically and seek an ally in psychoanalytic theory, a method that can in its affinity with philosophy add a necessary penetration to the thought already directed to tragedy. Psychoanalytic thought, grounded in philosophical problems generated by art and culture, strengthens as it enlarges philosophical interpretations of tragedy.

1

Psychoanalytic thought shares with tragedy a concern for the *dynamic* and *developmental* relationship between perceiver and object, an ever-changing relationship in which object and perceiver travel through stages of maturation. The life-project of growing up in culture is faithfully realized in tragic representations in which the excitement of feeling coalesces around objects. The audience undergoes an affective maturation in theatrical experience; and this helps us to understand the force of catharsis, the descriptive term for clarifying, separating out, and getting centered upon the *right* emotion—a process that lasts throughout the play and is not confined to the end, as it is commonly thought Aristotle claimed.

The ancient enmity between poetry and philosophy of which Plato speaks so approvingly represses the genuine and determinate and unchanging *difference* between poetry and philosophy by pretending that philosophy has at its disposal as many affective instruments as does poetry. It does not. And in the contest Plato sponsors in the dialogues, the cultural reality drops away and is replaced by a philosopher's fantasy. That fantasy persists, for Plato is not the only philosopher to wrap the argumentative self in the mantle of artistic powers. And yet the inter-inanimation of philosophy and tragedy may allow philosophy to realize a full theory of the emotions, for tragedy offers to philosophical theory a range of objects and emotions that are not to be found in the philosophical repertoire. Tragedy addresses a conflict that goes to the heart of political life: the conflict between private psychological need and public political obligation. Because of this preoccupation, tragedy stands at the intersection of the psychological and the philosophical, where individual unconscious drives intersect with group behavior and political values. Philosophy attempts to analyze that intersection, but has succeeded more fully with the political than with the drives of psychological need.

The ancient symbiosis between poetry and philosophy which underlies Plato's not exactly ingenuous remark that between poetry and philosophy there is an ancient enmity, comes down to whether one feels antagonistic to the competitors on the psychic field of play, or whether one accepts alliances. Already, in Plato's crabby rejection of poetry we see the need to dig out the latent beneath the manifest: Plato is, as writer and thinker, deeply the poet, as he is deeply the philosopher. One masks the other; masks masking are all the show with a *philosopher* who writes tragic dialogues that are really dramas. Since Plato, we have received endowments from his literary descendants who revile tragedy yet cannot leave it alone: Augustine, Rousseau, and Tolstoy are as condemning as Plato.

To be critical and philosophical in a psychoanalytic way is to be *reconstructive* rather than *deconstructive*. I make the distinction because so much recent philosophy of art has been shaped by the strategies of French thought, and while that thought has not been antagonistic to psychoanalytic thought, it uses the theory in its own way. My strategy aims to be at once psychoanalytic *and* historical; the combination allows me to pay attention to objects rather than to artists and their psychological dispositions. I shall not be biographical or clinical, but simply interpretative of objects. I shall not indulge in the study often referred to as "pathography," which seeks to connect artists' psychological peculiarities to their works; nor is it my aim to delineate a parallel pathography of objects.

Since I am by training a philosopher and in recent years have studied aesthetic problems from a psychoanalytic perspective, it is gratifying for me to see the boundaries of psychoanalytic inquiry extended beyond the rather reductionistic applications of the past. I believe that the study of the fate of tragedy in modernity can now draw upon a sophisticated development of Freud's original efforts. I refer especially to the writings of Ernst Kris, Leo Steinberg, Richard Wollheim, D. W. Winnicott, André Green, and Paul Ricoeur, among others, whose studies of the arts are informed by an appreciation of philosophical issues. If tragedy can be said to *be* anything other than what it obviously is, that *being* is philosophical. In general, the arts think philosophically, and throughout Western history, philosophy has relied heavily upon the arts.

If tragedy is philosophical, is philosophy ever tragic? I argue that it is, and that in modernity there are hidden aspects of the tragic in philosophical thought where we might overlook its deeper presence. Modernity seems incapable of creating tragic enactments, yet modernity exhibits a highly sensitive, though latent, awareness of tragedy in its traditional forms, reworking it into modern representations that appear, however, to be far removed from tragedy. Our eccentricity is to reform tragedy by denying it.

And that has been the experience of my generation: we in America have carried the inherited split between overt optimism and covert pessimism right into and through some of the bloodiest combat among nations. Yet those wars did end, and tragedy spoke directly to the survivors.

I

When the veterans of World War II returned to the universities, it was as if the cultures of Europe and Asia entered with them. Our nation would never return to its prewar insularity and cultural parochialism. The erosion of the "American" consciousness had been going on for some time—ever since the Civil War sent young men away from their home regions to distant states. World War II veterans confronted a different but no less radical change, for they had been preceded by an army of intellectual émigrés, especially from Europe, and higher education in the United States had absorbed their methods, ideas, and culture. So it was that I encountered the European tradition in American education after fighting through Europe, a veteran graduate student in Berkeley, California. That educational background influenced my way of thinking philosophically and my response to the goals philosophy set for itself in the postwar period. The positivistic doctrine that was imported was a reaction against the extravagances of Continental metaphysics. I carried within me—in large measure because of my wartime experience—a skepticism about this kind of positivistic philosophical analysis as I saw it pursued; and my dissatisfaction led me on a search for a wider, humanistic use and function to extend a tradition grown narrow and rigid. I had chosen as my graduate school one in which the influence of positivism had displaced indigenous philosophical thought: William James, George Santayana, John Dewey, and even C. S. Peirce had been put on the back shelf, and brought forward were Carnap, Reichenbach, Tarski (one of my teachers), and especially Schlick, whose visit to Berkeley as a professor of philosophy shortly before the war had a formative influence on a departmental point of view. The state of American philosophy at that time was one of dependency colored by a sense of inferiority: the analytic and positivistic movements from abroad had been internalized as the only way to "do" philosophy, as we used to say.

However, my own preparation to "do" philosophy prior to entering graduate school included not only the wartime experience, but also my earlier experience as an undergraduate student, when I became aware of the philosophical aspects of poetry and literature. I was fortunate to be able to work with the philosopher Philip Wheelwright, whose capacity to read the philosophical depths of the arts—poetry in particular—and yet to be rigorous about logic, ethics, and metaphysics, enabled me to sustain a self-preserving breadth right through a positivistic training. In 1944 I had left for a war in Europe, thinking about the war of Homer and Aeschylus; and in London I scoured the higgledy-piggledy piles of books in the basements of bomb-protected bookstores, finding among others the odd yet poetically useful translation—of sorts—of the *Agamemnon* by Louis McNiece. That went with me through the fighting, read in cellars and bunkers, thought about and dreamed over, until I returned. My first book[1] made use of that preoccupation and allowed me to bring together a past and a present, as I have tried to do here once again in the following chapters.

Through intimacy with the metaphorically complex vision of the *Oresteia*, I became aware of the deep political strains in classical tragedy; the present study carries that forward into modernity. It is the tragic destiny of tragedy that I have described and attempted to understand as a part of the world we have made, building on the past, but with a violence of our own that we have not been able to confront, as ancient civilization did—perhaps because our time is so much more dire and dreadful than any that has gone before. Nevertheless, it is clear: tragedy as a mode of representation of a cultural reality never disappears; it is transmitted to modernity and to the New World in strange and uncanny masks.

II

Tragedy as an art form of the classical world was buried during those middle centuries when Christianity condemned pagan shows, preferring the hope of resurrection to the wanhope of fate. Tragedy was reborn in the Elizabethan cultural exploration that celebrated and revivified dramatic enactments of the ancient world. Today

1. Richard Kuhns, *The House, the City, and the Judge: The Growth of Moral Awareness in the "Oresteia"* (Indianapolis: Bobbs-Merrill Co., 1962).

we keep both ancient and Elizabethan traditions alive in our classrooms and theaters; Aeschylus, Sophocles, and Shakespeare have their names chiseled into library facades so that we may monumentally mourn their memory. Nevertheless, cast into stone, the names suffer repression; we tend to think tragedy dead. That was Nietzsche's thought, to be followed by his vain and lovelorn hope that Wagnerian opera would establish a rebirth in modernity. But the way of tragedy in modernity is more complex. Indeed, like the repressed, it returns in strange and often deforming guises. The essays here devoted to modernity (chapters 4, 5, and 6 and the Epilogue) are to be understood as studies in unmasking.

I begin in chapter 1 by reflecting on Aeschylus' *Persians*, a dramatic monument that both founds and helps us to understand the contemporary memorials erected in so many of our cities and towns to our own tragic loss of youth in warfare. Drama and sculpture coalesce in the Vietnam Memorial in Washington, D.C., and I ask the reader to think of the relationship between drama and sculpture as the story unfolds, telling us of the wartime losses represented in the tragic drama acted at Athens. Aeschylus' *Persians* is perhaps the earliest of tragic dramas; poignant, moving, and terrifying, it creates the metaphor of fate in human form. Because we moderns have a tendency to interpret tragedy as cosmic inevitabilities and to see tragic heroes as in some odd sense innocent, it behooves us in our thinking to bring tragedy back to one of its political sources, warfare; and to one of its psychological sources, the family.

In the ancient tradition, which parceled out tragedy and comedy to seasonal occasions, the metaphysical implications for each genre were clear and distinct. But that was not the case when tragedy reappeared on the Elizabethan stage; comedy and tragedy could now occupy the same dramatic space. This permitted a multidimensional presentation of character and a complexity of plot unknown to Athens. In examining the tragic substructure that supports comedy, I have chosen to analyze, in chapter 2, Shakespeare's *The Merchant of Venice*. My purpose here is to expose hidden tragic depths and to demonstrate ways in which the play explores tragic experience through a paratragical plot. The *Merchant* is lightly flavored with melancholy and with various forms of mourning; though it laughs them off, we can see the underlying seriousness of these elements if we look closely at the characters and the language of this most entertaining drama.

Turning to the question posed by Aristotle, What is the pleasure peculiar to tragedy? (chapter 3), I explore and bring to bear on this question psychological concepts derived from psychoanalytic theory. Although Aristotle's theory of catharsis provided a psychological defense of tragedy, it did not seek to explain some of the deeper psychological sources of the need to perform tragic enactments. Freud's early formulation of the theory of catharsis, was also limited in its capacity to help us to understand the pleasure peculiar to tragedy. His later theoretical formulations, the development of the structural model, provide concepts that are more adequate to gaining an insight into the complexity of response to dramatic art. I elaborate three dynamic elements in tragedy: the riddle, psychosexual conflict, and splitting. These integral and related elements underlie the force and pleasure of our response to tragedy.

In chapter 4 I look at the search for tragedy in modernity, a period of which it has often been said that tragedy is an unlikely, if not an impossible form. This human experience transforms but never gives up its basic modes of representation. When the optimistic vision of the eighteenth-century Enlightenment banished tragic sensibilities to a position peripheral to the joys of life—joys which, it was believed, would be intensified by unstoppable advances in politics and knowledge—tragedy went underground. That retreat, truly a repression, persisted throughout nineteenth-century scientism. Our sense of ourselves was obscured. And yet our psychic histories do not change; tragic insights were everywhere to be found. We believe that *we* change as our forms of governance and economy move into their modern styles, but in reality—that is, the deepest psychic reality—human conditions of psychosexual development and familial conflict change but little. We may think ourselves in a "modern," or more likely "postmodern," posture, protected from ancient faults and remembered indignities; but the truth tragedy tells is that we cannot protect ourselves, neither through the wisdom of self-control nor through the magic of wish. There is no defense against the self in its fate. Though philosophy, exemplified in the writings of Immanuel Kant, argued its protective wisdom with its disavowal of metaphysical claptrap, within

7

this optimistic manifesto there yet lurked the inevitable tragic reality, to be uncovered and raised up like Lazarus. The dear, deadly-dark secret is ever present, even in the drawing room of modernity. The Enlightenment's elevation of reason, which carried within itself the seeds of the undoing of its own repression, allowed Heinrich Heine, in his genius, to understand the hidden riddles of modernity in their philosophical and literary expressions:

> Die Gestalt der wahren Sphinx
> Weicht nicht ab von der des Weibes;
> Faselei ist jener Zusatz
> Des betatzten Löwenleibes.
>
> Todesdunkel ist das Rätsel
> Dieser wahren Sphinx. Es hatte
> Kein so schweres zu erraten
> Frau Jokastens Sohn und Gatte.
>
> Doch zum Glücke kennt sein eignes
> Rätsel nicht das Frauenzimmer;
> Spräch es aus das Lösungswort,
> Fiele diese Welt in Trümmer.
>
> (The figure of the real Sphinx
> Is not different from a woman's;
> It is incoherent, the composite
> Lion-body with the claws.
>
> Deadly dark is the riddle
> Of the true Sphinx.
> Frau Jocasta's son and husband
> Did not have to solve such a difficult one.
>
> But it's lucky that the riddle
> Is not possessed by the lady;
> For if she spoke the solution,
> The world would fall into ruins.)

(Zum Lazarus, no. 9)

Moving to a powerful exemplification of the Kantian moral universe in chapter 5, I study the quest for justice that consumes one of the great characters in modern linguistic art, Michael Kohlhaas. Kleist, a great reader of Kant, inverts and subverts tragic plots and characters in a way so radical that we are endowed with a new kind of experience that reinterprets tragedy and establishes an artistic reality to shape the modern sensibility. Antigone's ghostly presence reverberates incongruously in the figure seen on the landscape of the Peasant Wars of central Europe.

Crossing the Atlantic, in chapter 6, to the New World, to America, we find nineteenth-century frontier bravado overlying a deep pessimism, a contradiction of feeling that matches the darkness of Kleist's vision. Melville and Kleist are fit for each other's bitterness and sense of tragic irresolvabilities lying hidden in the core of ordinary experience of ordinary people. In *The Confidence Man,* Melville creates a philosophical and psychological analysis to lay bare a New World full of contradictions and repressions. His insights into the paradox of the liar, matching those of present-day logicians, become a part of the higher biblical criticism, as he restates the case for tragic nihilism in our frontier behavior.

I conclude my discussion of the evolution of tragedy from mourning to repression with reflections on two American poets whose ways with tragedy have been for the most part overlooked. Walt Whitman, who knew of psychological necessities that torture the stages of development in a child's growing up, sought a solution in public celebration of the body. For Emily Dickinson, before the private altar of the self, the springs of unconscious desire are disclosed in torrid symbols; the body has its way with the mind, whatever defenses consciousness throws in its path. Through art and poetry, each of these poets in their different ways celebrates an apotheosis of the senses as the true resurrection. While American linguistic art draws upon a past represented in America's own indigenous forms, it yet recognizes a continuity of tragic falls as grievous, as deep, as mournful as any bewept in history.

1 Loss and Mourning in Aeschylus' *Persians*

> Our bodies cannot love:
> But, without one,
> What works of Love could we do?
> W. H. Auden

American wartime losses have been endured with little of the demonstrative mourning we are exposed to in ancient Greek tragedy. Yet recently Americans, too, have found a way to mourn their wartime dead even though lacking a national theater. The design and location of the Vietnam Memorial in Washington, D.C. provides a place and an occasion; Americans can be seen in public demonstrations of grief. Opposition to establishing such a place was aroused, in part, by bureaucratic anxiety over just this kind of expression. Americans ought to keep their mourning to themselves. Only primitive peoples express their mourning in display and emotion. Certainly the Athenians were unrestrained; imagine a whole city sitting through a play such as *The Persians*, first performed in Athens in 472 B.C. as a ritual recognition of Greek victory over invading barbarians, the Persians under the generalship of Xerxes.

The Persians has always been admired as a dramatic tour de force: that a Greek writer could project upon an Athenian stage the scene of far-off Susa strikes us as artistically daring and politically empathetic, even inexplicably generous. This way of seeing the action, which ties it to the other, the vanquished enemy, appears to overlook the play's immediate audience and their own complicity in the process of mourning. Persians mourn; so do Athenians; so do we. *The Persians* is not simply a scene in Susa; it is a representation of a universal expression of grief over the disappearance of a city's young men.

11

For our part today, because we wish to avoid painful representations, the process and condition of mourning pose difficulties. Until the Vietnam Memorial came into our national life, we tended to cope with wartime deaths by distancing, or we tried to rationalize the suffering of those who had fallen. We carried this disposition over into our readings of *The Persians.* Thus we said, *The Persians* is *about* loss and the grief of distant people in Susa, *of course* they are mourning; their leader as good as abducted the youth of Susa for a distant escapade that exhibits infatuation, and the Greeks were civilized people who recognized political suicide, as this drama clearly demonstrates . . . or something like that. In giving ourselves such accounts we soften the harshness of the drama and the pain of our own mourning, so that we watch the play without undue passion. We console ourselves in this very case by separating ourselves from *barbaric* postures! However, if closely attended, *The Persians* forbids ameliorations; it forces the audience to confront mourning by drawing the audience into that very process. How the play achieves this is one concern in the following discussion.

My method will be largely psychoanalytic because the theory draws us close to all that we find in this drama: to dreams, to mourning, to family constellations, to male and female conduct in actions of aggression, to the memorializing of the past and anticipations of future moral stature. I rely upon the psychoanalytic method not because I believe it to be always the best and most fruitful; in some cases it does little to open up the inner being of art. But in this case I think it does help us to move from manifest to latent content in both the historical telling and the character portrayal. Psychoanalytic inquiry must come to grips with the historical as this play gives it to us, and I hope that my effort at interpretation will show that art can be used to enlighten and deepen theory. When a theory is brought to bear on a work of art, both must benefit. Theory lets us see more deeply into art; art helps to define, articulate, and sharpen theory. Thus as *we* move through history, future interpretations ought to benefit from past interpretations. Our interpretative response to and our deep feeling towards *The Persians* will help us to develop appropriate responses to tragedy in its modern disguises. So in the chapters that follow I shall be in constant recollection of *The Persians;* the art of Aeschylus is deeply philosophical, as it is psychologically sensible and spacious.

I

The Persians can be watched as an unfolding of time in several of its culture dimensions: historical, generational, and individual. Most basic to plot structure is historical time—the events that lead up to the expedition against Greece, the loss of the Persian army and navy, and the return of the survivor(s) to Susa. We say that those events *really* happened, as set over against the rising of Darius from his tomb and the posture of Xerxes on his return. Set within historical time is the time of the performance of the play that we, the audience, watch. Odd as that sounds, it states the artistic reality: we who witness the action are embedded in historical time ourselves. Yet as we watch we become aware of a time that coerces both historical time and dramatic time: that is the plot time, which may extend far beyond history or may compress history into a tale told by a herald who walks on from a distant place; and plot time may be not all coincident with enactment time, the actual time it takes to play the play. One way to look upon these temporal levels, which pass one another like voices in a fugue, is as lines of force that sprout out from a magnet's poles to return to the magnet in a constant recirculation. Lines of force run both independently and in concert with other lines of force; sometimes they pair up to run concurrently and side by side. Certainly events in Greece and in Persia are "yoked together" for the duration of the enactment and before and after the enactment. And the fighters on the two sides will be locked together in living combat and will lie together in a field strewn with their bodies. These conditions of temporal organization in which history, cultures, and persons are paired suggest to the poet his most powerful and his ever-present metaphor: the yoke, yoking. This metaphor holds within its grasp both the grand sweep of history and private psychological drives to coerce and to love.

We meet the metaphor in the introductory choral ode, alongside its plaintive companion (its yoke-fellow), the word gone/lost. Thus *oixomenon* (gone/lost) and *amphiballo* (to encompass, to embrace) sound like a bass figured throughout the opening verses. The deeper of the two, and most important in my reading, is the action of surrounding (*amphiballo*) in the extended meaning of to encompass and to embrace, for it is joined to the word *zygon* (yoke). And the central force in the action is "yoking" in all its applications.

13

The verb *amphiballo* and its cognates cover activities such as wrapping, throwing a covering around (as clothing), embracing, and, when joined to *zygon*, yoking. By metaphoric extension it connotes enslavement, surrounding as in battle, and the postures of physical love. Thus there is a basic ambivalence in the term: to join as in combat—to join as in love. The term "yoke" generically means to pair under a confining device or restraint, as oxen are yoked when pulling a plow. As we know from English usage, yoke has metaphorical meanings that reach out to marriage and to punishment. Captives are yoked; slaves are yoked; wedded couples are "yoked." Several of these meanings are packed into Shakespeare's thought: "Think every bearded fellow that's but yoak'd may draw with you?" (*Othello*, 4.1). And in the nasty remark by Thersites in *Troilus and Cressida*, I read a hidden reference to *The Persians*: "There's Ulysses and Nestor . . . yoke you like draught oxen, and make you plow up the wars" (2.2). Equally drawn to the power of the action and the device, Aeschylus uses "yoking" in a set congruent with the Elizabethan metaphoric range: in *The Persians* alone the term will serve for combat, love, marriage, politics, and infatuation with power.

A concept so rich in metaphoric extensions serves the action of *Persians* well: Xerxes attempts to "yoke" two cultures, an act of violation; the youth of Susa (and Athens) are "yoked" to death, as if that be their marriage portion. If we extend the metaphor to our own military exploits into other cultures, this aspect of "yoking" arouses painful reflections that are not within the historical setting of *The Persians*. Now, as then, yoking may be beneficent or malevolent; it is difficult for human beings bent to their private goals to distinguish the two sides of the pairing. This deep ambivalence is given vivid representation as soon as Atossa reveals her dream:

> Two women as an apparition came,
> One in Persian robes instructed well,
> The other Doric, both in splendor dressed,
> Who grand and most magnificent excelled
> Us now, their beauty unreproached, spotless;
> Sisters they, who casting for their father's land,
> She Greece received, she Asia, where to dwell.
> Then strife arose between them, or so I dreamed;
> And my son, observing this, tries to check

And soothe them; he yokes them to a chariot,
Bridles their necks: and one, so arrayed, towers
Proud, her mouth obedient to reins;
But the other stamps, annoyed, and rends apart
Her trappings in her hands; unbridled, seizes
The car and snaps its yoke in two;
My son falls, and his father, pitying,
Stands by his side, but at whose sight Xerxes
Tears his robes. Thus in the night these visions
Dreamed: but when, arisen, I touched the springs'
Fair-flowing waters, approached the altar, wishing
To offer sacrifice religiously
To guardian deities, whose rites these are,
Then to Phoebus' hearth I saw an eagle fleeing:
Dumb in dread I stood: a falcon swooped
Upon him, its wings in flight, its claws plucked
At his head: he did no more than cower, hare-like.
Those were my terrors to see, and yours to hear.
My son, should he succeed, would be admired;
But if he fails, Persia cannot hold him
To account. Whichever comes, safe returned, sovereign
He shall rule.[1]

Historically and culturally the two cultures cannot pull together; they are yoked mistakenly by Xerxes' imperialist ambition. His failure shatters Atossa's maternal idealization of her son, and both parents watch as the child falls, then tears his robes at the sight of his father. The act is one at once of desperation, shame, and mourning. The dream hides within it two fantasies, paired generational delusions: the parents' fantasy of their child's perfection and power and wholeness, covering him with a narcissistic mantle that he wears and attempts to divest himself of; and the child's fantasy of parental power verging on omnipotence and thus clothing them in a might he cannot live up to and must fail to achieve even though he attempts mighty deeds. Parents and child are clothed by misrepresentations in the unconscious evaluation of each

---

1. Aeschylus, *The Persians*, trans. S. G. Benardete, lines 181–214, in *Aeschylus II*, ed. David Grene and Richmond Lattimore (Chicago: University of Chicago Press, 1956). All quotations are from this translation.

other, and the act of rending takes on extended meanings. The mourning ritual of rending clothing is both a gesture of mourning and the expression of a wish—even a need—to be divested of that false mantle in which one is enwrapped by the other. To be clothed and to be divested extends the yoke metaphor to cover the child-parent relationship: Darius, Atossa, and Xerxes are "yoked" together as parents and child, as older and younger generations incapable of "pulling together," just as are the women who represent Greece and Persia in Atossa's dream. The being harnessed to one chariot is an obvious metaphor we see repeated in Plato's *Phaedrus* myth of the white horse and the black horse, who if uncontrolled may pull the chariot off its course. In each case the drive either falls or masters the two beasts. Indeed, there is a certain continuity between the chariot metaphor as a model of the soul and the chariot metaphor as a model for the family constellation.

Beginning my comments by reference to historical movement and conflict through time, I have shifted to the latent content of the dream dreamt by the woman who dominates the drama, the woman who stands with the chorus—men of the city—bereft, longing, crying out to the dead as they hope against hope they may welcome back the living. Historical time moves inexorably towards doom. The fated outcome, in which the Persians must lose their flower of youth, is itself yoked to the father-son succession. Fate here, as in primordial myths, expresses itself through father-son succession; we have been given a hint of that already in the mother's dream. Xerxes' insane exploit to yoke two cultures follows from a competitive need in the son, and the source of the need is made clear to us through the words of the ghost of the father, Darius, risen from the tomb.

We today, living in the post-Elizabethan age as we live in the postclassical age, cannot help but think of old Hamlet and his appearance to the son, as we encounter Darius and his ectoplasmic pronouncements aimed at *his* son. *Hamlet* could be taken—for an anachronistic moment—as a model for *The Persians*; Shakespeare's drama prevails upon the audience to mourn and to learn to mourn. We see in the father-son succession two stages of the development towards generational accommodation: first the *inability* to mourn, followed by a mourning so devastating that the mourners themselves must perish.

Now moving back in time to *The Persians,* we are solicited by that drama to bear witness to mourning: first to overcome our *inability* to mourn, then to learn through watching the process whereby mourning not only can occur, but in occurring encourages development out of a deficiency and inability to mourn towards a higher and more complex maturity of psychological and moral development. This process of moving from deficiency to mastery through mourning is the latent content of the manifest story of Xerxes' return. The story of Xerxes could be told thus: a youth become an ancient through adventures psychosexually depicted as a family drama, yet at the same time a family drama within a political drama. The history of political action and the history of psychic life intertwine to drive the infatuated leader into another culture where he is fated to fail, for boundaries both political and psychological have been overstepped.

The story is told with great stretches of silence, punctuated by the cries of mourning. There is much breathless anticipation as we wait for news. This is one side of warfare. The other side occupies a closely related play by Aeschylus, *Seven Against Thebes,* in which the clang and clamor of preparation for war resounds throughout the action. The play is filled with armor clashing, women howling, the city in turmoil. In the two plays political action mirrors internal psychic movement, and psychic life generates political action. Taken together, the two plays drive home a deep truth of tragedy: the conflict between public political obligation and private psychic need is inevitable and never to be reconciled in a proper yoking. The wisdom that comes through suffering—a trope in tragedy's comment upon itself—comes at a cost that renders the wisdom useless and empty, for human beings are doomed to repetition.

To be sure, Xerxes learns to mourn, at the cost of sacrificing a whole generation of young men. Originally, his need to engage in the generational abduction was derived from his familial conflicts—his father's success, his mother's hopes—as the familial conflicts prevented his being able to mourn, when mourning was appropriate, at the death of Darius. How to mourn, then, begins at the tomb of the father, Darius, and we must attend to that moving scene to understand Xerxes' infatuation. The ghost tells us about the interwoven strands of impulse that led to Xerxes' expedition and the entombment of multitudes whose ghosts will forever remain silent. To understand the dark Darius' dismal discourse we need preparation, so I shall set the stage for his appearance.

We learn of the Persian defeat and Xerxes' shame in lines 466–72, delivered by the herald. The loss is devastating: "Thus the city of Persians / May lament, regretting the loss of youth." The chorus responds by interpreting the deaths in erotic metaphors: "Wedded but lately / Couches forsaken . . ." This interweaving of love and death compares the body sated, as it were, in death with the body sated in love. We are familiar with this thematic interweaving, but the Greek poets developed it in elegant variations.[2]

Because *The Persians* presents its witnesses with a loss that surpasses ordinary separation by death—the dread mowing down of youth, slowly realized as the action unfolds—the men of the chorus must struggle to join love to death. They must draw upon a submerged net of memories, images, and inherited ways to represent death that are even more primitive than those that the fifth-century Athenians had consciously available. It is this reaching down to the depths of mourning and the ways in which it is to be represented that gives this play its awful power. For ordinarily—if there is any "ordinary" surrounding death—families who lose youths and maidens to death before they can be joined in love and marriage find consolation in memorial rites that tradition allows, a play-acting union in the other world, the realm of death. But the devastation of war, the cutting down of youthful lives in warfare, makes that fantasy—that dreary, although perhaps consoling, union in Hades—difficult to sustain. A terrible consequence of war is that no obsequies are sufficient or in any way consoling. The mythology and the rituals of death must be suspended, or, in desperate need of some way to lay to rest those who are forever gone—and physically *nowhere*—a substitute ritual of mourning must be empowered. It is the search for this displacement of mourning usually attached to the dead body, to something other, an *other object*, that drives the Persian men in an effort to come to terms with their loss. The sweet youthful presence, even in a corpse, is denied them.

2. The best discussion of the classical love/death theme is in Emily Vermeule, *Aspects of Death in Early Greek Art and Poetry* (Berkeley: University of California Press, 1981), chap. 5, "On the Wings of the Morning: Pornography of Death."

Therefore, the rich mythology of death is in this drama cut back, confined, filtered, even, I would say, subjected to catharsis in its root sense of separating out, confining the gestures and words of mourning to the essence of mourning, as it were. And that is one reason the play has often been slighted: the play itself is in an essential sense *slight*— that is to say, in it mourning is as it is essentially. There are few references to the mythology of death, but rather a displacement of this mythology onto the repeated metaphors. Thus in the few lines below, the longings of death are expressed through *yoke, bed,* and *pothos.* Here is Emily Vermeule's description of *pothos:* "*Pothos* is generally a feeling of longing in the nighttime for someone who is not there, a lover gone overseas, or the absent dead."[3] *Pothos* is apparent in the sighing, singing, and anxious anticipations of the chorus as they await word of the expedition whose mad purpose was yoking, and whose unwanted result was to leave one alone in the yoke:

> All the horse and infantry
> Like a swarm of bees have gone
> With the captain of the host,
> Who joined the headlands of either land,
> Crossing the yoke of the sea.
>
> Beds with longing fill with tears,
> Persian wives in softness weep;
> Each her armed furious lord
> Dismissed with gentle love and grief,
> Left alone in the yoke.

(122–39)

Pothos directs our thoughts to the dead and is a denier of sleep to those who mourn. It accompanies the irresistible need to weep as one is mourning.

In the choral song that opens the drama (1–155), Aeschylus creates a deeply moving identification of the loss of youth with the embrace of love; once again we are forced to recognize yoking in its two aspects. This recognition is followed by the raising of Darius, once the husband of Atossa, from his "bed," his tomb (623–80). Part of our recognition is

---

3. Ibid., 154.

that the royal couple were lovers and are to be compared to the young men—never to return to their couches of love, but, like Darius, forever to lie in death's relaxation.

II

The psychoanalytic understanding of mourning and death helps us to see into the philosophical and psychological depths of Aeschylus' drama. To mourn and to love are congruent conditions and processes imposing a burden upon individuals and communities that may crush them. The insight of psychoanalysis is this: in mourning and in love a task is imposed upon libido and upon the attachment persons have, through libido, to objects. A long process of working through is undertaken. The outcome for the mourner is detachment from the object; for the lover, attachment to the object. In both cases, the process requires repetition over time, a recognition exhibited to the audience through *The Persians'* stressed return to the posture and the sounds of mourning. Kurt Eissler gives a psychoanalytic description that reveals the dramatic strategies underlying the plot of *The Persians:*

> In the process of mourning a certain work is performed upon all representations of an object that the mourner has lost forever. Mourning consists of the repetition of the same psychological acts, applied, however, to a variety of contents. The work the ego does in the process of mourning consists in turning towards the recollections, fantasies, or wishes directly or indirectly associated with the lost object's image. . . .
>
> . . . two affects so different as mourning and loving have one factor in common. Subjects prepossessed by them concentrate with all their thoughts, words, and actions upon a partner, repeat the same process, and assume that the partner to whom these repetitions are devoted responds with positive feelings. For the mourner too will if asked give assurance that the person lost by death would be happy to know that the mourner's mind is filled with the image of the deceased.[4]

4. Kurt Eissler, *Goethe: A Psychoanalytic Study, 1775–1786*, 2 vols. (Detroit: Wayne State University Press, 1963), 658–60.

The drama presented to the Athenian audience provides evidence of the mourners' preoccupation, but also—and here the *dramatic* reality becomes *psychologically* and *politically* efficacious—endows the audience with a representation that stands as an object upon which great emotional force can be exerted. Eissler continues:

> The mourning person . . . does not know where to put his libido. It is still bound to the representation of the lost person, but he knows that it cannot rest there, or, if it does, that it is really attached to an illusion, so to speak, to something that does not exist in reality. Yet illusions are pleasurable only when we are not aware that they are illusions—at least at the moment when they fill our minds. If the mourner could forget for one moment that his strivings were directed towards a deceased person he would feel like a passionate lover.[5]

Underlying this identification of death and love, of deceased and beloved, is the unconscious wish that death's fearsomeness might be transformed into the pleasure of sexual union and slackening. Thus the dreaded is transformed into that to be sought, pain metamorphosed into pleasure. This wish was explored by Freud in his essay "The Theme of the Three Caskets," which postulates an underlying latent content to the myth of the hero who chooses the beautiful woman; through her silence she is understood to represent death. Death is transformed into the most desirable and by association into the physically gratifying. This deepest wish finds conscious representation, Freud argued, in many myths. Our mythic representation of the expedition against Greece in *The Persians* provides another instance of the human mind's transformational powers in the face of cultural disaster. So youths lost on both sides, in Susa and in Athens, are united with the love object; tomb metamorphosed into couch.

I have arrived at last at the tomb of Darius, where one dramatic and philosophical function of the scene is to prepare the audience for the identifications maintained in our deepest unconscious wish that to be embraced by death is to embrace the beautiful love object. Through this

5. *Ibid.*

scene unconscious wishes become conscious, manifest objects that the audience confronts, and in its shocked gaze comes to recognize a terrible contradiction: that our poetic expressions are at once denials *and* recognitions of the truth of our infatuated, aggressive acts. The scene at the tomb, then, centers the action as *tragic* action, for tragic action is best defined as representation and recognition of unresolvable contradictions. Follow the ritual of invocation:

The father Darius is assured of the love borne him (647–48) as due the parents and leaders gone; thus ought the living to feel towards all fathers now that they are dead. And Darius makes his appearance as an answer to the force of love, as if only love could have pulled him up from the underworld: "Ascent is not easy / The chthonic deities more readily / Receive than give" (688–90). Darius then reviews Xerxes' excesses: the spring of evil action is found in the naive effort to yoke the waters and the cultures through youthful ignorance and pride (742–46). The father ends his vituperations with the typical parental comment: "Had not my son diseased his sense? / I fear my labored wealth will fall the prey / Of conquerors." Atossa, again typically, replies that her son was misadvised and misled by wicked men who contrasted Darius' success in war with Xerxes' passivity. Of course Xerxes had to prove himself!

Although it appears at first that the father blames while the mother defends, the father's final words are a directive to the mother to meet the son whose clothing is rent, to sooth him with words that, as they come from the mother, will be heeded.

> And you, aged
> Mother of Xerxes, go to the palace;
> Gather up rich and brilliant cloths, and go
> To meet your son; for he, in grief, has rent
> His embroidered robes to shreds. Gently soothe
> Him with your words: to yours alone he'll listen.
>
> (832–37)

Parental care extends so far as to defend the son even in this debacle. But soon we shall watch Xerxes come before us in his mourning posture, and then the deepest truth of the action will be available to us: we may at last gain access to a truth I shall attempt to bring up from the latent unconscious—the tomb, as it were—to manifest awareness. The nether realm holds many ghosts whose powers may be invoked.

I think *The Persians* may help us to understand that cryptic hypothesis of Freud's theory: the superego is heir to the Oedipus complex. And once we understand Freud's words, the deepest levels of *The Persians* should begin to appear.

Freud will go on to explore this principle in several places; its last assertion is found in the unfinished "An Outline of Psychoanalysis," where he says, "The superego is in fact the heir to the Oedipus complex and is only established after that complex has been disposed of."[6] In his late essay *The Ego and the Id*, the principle is stated as follows: "The ego ideal is therefore the heir of the Oedipus complex, and thus it is also the expression of the most powerful impulses and the most important libidinal vicissitudes of the id."[7] In "The Economic Problem of Masochism," Freud writes, ". . . [the] superego is as much a representative of the id as of the external world. It came into being . . . through . . . the introjection into the ego of the parents. . . ."[8] Then, in an expansion of the idea, mythic elements are connected to the parental identification: "The last figure in the series that began with the parents is the dark power of Destiny which only the fewest of us are able to look upon as impersonal."[9] Greek tragedy, we might think, reverses the order: "the dark power of Destiny" generates the action, and the last figure in the series is the parents. Setting ancient and modern modes of representing destiny side by side, as obverse and reverse of one lifelong entanglement, allows us to recognize (and this is *tragic* recognition) the latent content in *The Persians*.

To make the comparison helpful, we must be able to sustain a cultural comparison as we think about the psychoanalytic theory of superego development. In Greek tragedy, destiny (Moira, fate, one's portion in life, the necessity that structures cosmic order) hovers over the action;

---

6. Sigmund Freud, "An Outline of Psychoanalysis," in *Standard Edition of the Complete Psychological Works of Sigmund Freud*, ed. James Strachey (London: Hogarth Press, 1953–74), 23:205. (Hereafter cited as *Std. Ed.*)

7. Freud, *The Ego and the Id*, in *Std. Ed.*, 19:36.

8. Freud, "The Economic Problem of Masochism," in *Std. Ed.*, 19:167.

9. Ibid., 168.

but beneath the action we see the familial psychosexual conflicts. In contrast, we today begin with the developmental stages of the individual in the family and only later come to imagine a fate that hovers over us. Thus Freud's statement—that destiny for us is displaced from its traditional impersonal force and comes to be anchored in the familial, yet can again in our consciousness be seen as impersonal—takes on a mysterious, dark quality. How are we to understand Freud's statement? Freud invokes the self-evident truth of Greek tragedy: destiny rules us, as it rules all human life. That understanding was evident in classical drama; but today few of us can face that reality, and therefore we tend to deflect the truth or to ameliorate its harshness in ways that the Athenian dramatists did not have to resort to. Saying it this way pulls Freud's observation close to Nietzsche's insight which seems most apt to our reflections on *The Persians*: "It was through tragedy that myth achieved its profoundest content, its most expressive form; it arose again like a wounded warrior, its eyes alight with unspent power and the calm wisdom of the dying." Freud never writes with the poetic frenzy of Nietzsche, yet underneath Freud's staid prose is a wild insight: that those things we speak of psychoanalytically can be spoken of in another language, now lost to us except in the Dionysian insights of great tragedy. "The Dionysiac truth," writes Nietzsche, "appropriates the entire realm of myth as symbolic language for its own insights, which it expresses partly in the public rite of tragedy and partly in the secret celebration of dramatic mysteries, but always under the old mythic veil."[10] Watching *The Persians*, we participate in a public rite of tragedy, but it has secret depths in which the celebrations of mourning go on. Freud's exploration of the connection between mourning and the establishment of the superego brings into consciousness a latent depth; the distinction between the underlying myth and the public rite now comes into our experience. Freud saw in tragedy the complement to his clinical discoveries, and in turn those discoveries help us in our understandings of tragedy.

To plumb the depths of *The Persians*, it will be helpful to consider action from within the drama (as a function of character) and from

---

10. Friedrich Nietzsche, *The Birth of Tragedy*, trans. Francis Golffing (New York: Anchor Books, 1956), section 10.

without the drama (as a function of audience). I want to explore the underlying psychological conditions that make mourning possible, the ways in which mourning comes to fruition, as it were. How does the ability to mourn supervene upon the inability to mourn?

The movement of *The Persians'* plot can be described as occupying a series of stages. The description I rely upon now is psychoanalytic in origin: the erring son, Xerxes, moves from pre-Oedipal immaturity, through Oedipal conflict, to superego maturation. In the final maturational moment, objects and norms originally associated with the parents are consciously recognized. The ultimate internalization of those objects and norms does not occur until the very end of the drama. My contention is that the *audience* accommodates the tragic recognitions through an internalization that is part of the dramatic process referred to as catharsis. And that process—psychological and political—endows the drama with a power to transform inability to mourn into ability to mourn.

Once I have given a description of tragic plot in terms of stages of moral development—as they would be thought through psychoanalytically—I think immediately of the plot analysis worked out in Aristotle's *Poetics*. Categories as simple and sensible as "beginning," "middle," and "end" encompass the possibility that plot moves towards consciousness as a maturational development. The psychosexual-functional stages investigated and mapped by Freud are in several respects coincident with the plot structure taken by Aristotle to be the best for tragedy, that is, the plot in which "reversal" and "recognition" occur. While it may appear strange to compare the two thinkers, it now seems to me that they agree in a developmental hypothesis: the psychoanalytic sees the psychosexual stages of maturation as the foundation for moral growth and insight, while the Aristotelian attributes moral self-consciousness to sequences of feeling and insight produced by an interaction between the well-constructed plot and the audience. Theatrical experience generated by a single drama can be likened to the process of growing up in culture.

The deep insights achieved in the *Poetics* derive from a suppressed other in the dramatic situation, that is, the audience. Aristotle does not list "audience" as one of the categories in the *Poetics*, but as soon as we study the terms in which plot, character, thought, diction, and the rest are analyzed, we see that all along Aristotle has been seeing in terms of both *plot* as enacted and *audience* as responsive. And this he must do if he is to place tragedy in its appropriate *political* setting. The dominant questions the *Poetics* seeks to answer are (1) in what way is tragedy *politically* justifiable (a search necessitated by Plato's view, which stands as a challenge and to which the *Poetics* is an answer, even a rebuttal); and (2) wherein lies the *pleasure* appropriate to tragedy?

Thus when I bring the plot of *The Persians* into the discussion, I see that the underlying plot of the play is the search implicit in all tragedy, precisely Aristotle's question, and precisely Freud's question in his ruminations on culture: In what structure of family and communal life may human beings find a stable political life? Therefore, one interesting way to classify Athenian tragedies is according to the kind of rule explored and how it is evaluated. It appears to be generally affirmed that rule through family inheritance leads to disaster. Blood ties and marriage ties are taken up for inspection, and the most wide-ranging drama in the exploration of this problem is Aeschylus' *Oresteia*, where husband-wife, woman–adulterous lover, and mother-son combinations, as well as single rule by male and by female, are all suggested in the complex political life of that trilogy. None work. In each case the overwhelming sexual force obliterates political stability. Tragedy's insight into this inevitable and ineradicable conflict led Plato to revise the whole family structure and sexual expectations in that part of the *Republic* devoted to the most daring renovations (Book 5). It is worth noting that when Socrates approaches the most delicate questions of family and sex, he slips into the mode of tragedy: "So I salute Nemesis [*Adrasteian*, or inevitability] in what I am about to say" (451A). Plato's anxieties about the destructive force of tragedy are to an extent well founded; it was Aristotle's purpose in the *Poetics* to undermine them. Whether or not Aristotle was as sensitive as Plato to the threats tragedy posed to political life we cannot say; but if we simply concentrate on the tragedies themselves, we can understand the origin of philosophy's first great dispute over the nature of art.

The *Oresteia* moves in its conclusion from an examination of human rule to the possibility of divine rule. In that wish-fulfilling finale, we see tragedy turning its power of resolution upon itself, suggesting an amelioration of its own harsh insights. Let the gods give guidance to political life; then shall we prosper, because under divine leadership the dreadful Furies will be transformed into Eumenides (Kindly Ones) and watch over the proper mating of women and men. If god-guided marriage becomes the sexual matrix, then political life will go well. It is an odd suggestion: that to grow up and to be mature sexually is the guarantee of political stability. Yet that is the deepest secret hidden in the *Oresteia*.

In contrast, tragedy that carries through to its own harsh conclusions avoids wish-fulfillments. We may see the difference if we set Sophocles' *Oedipus the King* alongside the *Oresteia*. For in *Oedipus* the full force of sexual-political contradiction must be borne by the audience. And it is that burden thrust upon us that calls for the psychological process of catharsis. Through catharsis the contradiction is to this extent resolved: that we the audience can offer to the doomed and polluted Oedipus an acceptance, though he be cast out of his community.

Turning now to the drama of central concern here, *The Persians*, we find tragedy exploring a third way to a political future, through the process of mourning. Xerxes was taken to be a god; he is brought down to (or rather, metamorphosed into) the human being he has been all along, but now cleansed of his infatuation and his political blindness. He, the lordly one, is overwhelmed by abject sorrow. The transformation is beautifully described by Helen Bacon:

> The climax of this final revelation of Xerxes as fallible mortal is visual as well as verbal and musical. The king of kings calls on the chorus to look on the remnants of his followers, . . . at his quiver almost emptied of arrows, at his torn garments, and finally cries, "I am stripped [literally 'naked,' *gumnos*] of my escort." The new escort that forms to conduct him to his palace is a ritual acknowledgement of his new, vulnerable, merely human state, the mourning chorus, on foot, beating their breasts, lacerating their cheeks, tearing their hair.
> . . . The new escort objectifies and sums up the new state of affairs, in which a semidivine king has been replaced by one who is human, fallible, vulnerable.[11]

11. Helen Bacon, "Aeschylus," in *Ancient Writers: Greece and Rome*, ed. T. James Luce (New York: Charles Scribner's, 1982), 1:120–21.

Close consideration of *The Persians* exposes tragic insights that are peculiar to this drama. From an Aristotelian point of view, reversal and recognition really have occurred before the action opens, and realistically enough, tragic knowledge comes from *historical reality* and not from myth. The Athenian audience already knows the outcome and the conditions under which the plot swerves—from blindness to insight—in the terrifying conflict between Eastern barbarian invaders and defending Greeks. Thus the denouement takes on a historical reference as it delivers a tragic moral insight. The observation made by Helen Bacon goes right to the tragic revelation: "a semidivine king has been replaced by one who is human, fallible, vulnerable." The audience *recognizes* the new status of the once-proclaimed God of Kings—that he is a mere (hence much-to-be-valued) human. This has been Athenian political wisdom all along: that the Greeks honor humanity in its humanness, while barbarians misplace veneration, elevating the human to divine status. That in itself is a tragic mistake. And it is a mistake the Athenians can appreciate politically, as it thereby allows them to mourn with and alongside the Persians. Now both communities mourn the loss of children that in this drama must (it is a narrative assumption) drive home to the Persians their infatuation in their political misidentity of man as God.

Left with the political understanding gained from the Persian expedition, all communities may construct a future out of their disastrous pasts, provided the human proportions of psychosexual maturation are internalized and nurtured. Nurturance comes from the polis rightly ruled; Plato saw that, as did Aristotle. But the difference between their visions is momentous: for Aristotle, it is through art as such, especially tragedy, that right rule may be understood (though there are companion philosophical ways to this end); and in *The Persians* it is through tragedy, rightly constructed, that a future may be built by yoking the positive emotion of mourning to the possibility of young women and men establishing an at-homeness for themselves in the city cleansed of its infatuations concerning war.

The beginning, middle, and end of the drama display an Aristotelian plot structure as well as a movement towards consciousness that conforms to the psychoanalytic description of maturational stages. The psychosexual stages investigated and mapped by Freud are, I maintain, coincident with tragic energies and events recognized in the theory Aristotle developed in his close examination of tragic structures. However, the propulsive force that Freud brings to our attention, and that later psychoanalytic observers have dwelt upon, is the process of mourning. It is precisely this process of mourning that I see in *The Persians* as the plot energy propelling events and revealing character; and it is this foundation of action that Aristotle leaves largely out of account. How is it that the process of mourning has the power to move this plot from beginning, through middle, to end?

It is now time for me to bring together the psychodynamic developmental process with the dramatic process in which a play is produced and performed—in short, to relate moral maturation to enactment. Through the aesthetic and the moral interconnections, we are able to draw from the drama insights into the process of mourning and to draw from psychoanalytic theory insights into the play itself. I shall retell the story of *The Persians* through a plot pattern expressed in psychoanalytic language, for that language describes a dramatic action subsumed by the manifest plot.

In the early encounters between Atossa and Darius, the couple exchange recollections and interpretations of their son's actions (as they do also in Atossa's dream). As we listen to the parents, one source of the tragic conflict that generates the dramatic plot becomes clear: the son was driven to overcome and to best the political achievement of the father. Xerxes' overweening need to triumph drove him to undertake the expedition against Greece, and the words spoken make it clear that his wish was not simply to beat threatening neighbors into submission, but also to do one better than the father, who was the real (if psychological) threat. The need to triumph in psychological terms (leaving aside for the moment political aims) foreclosed the process of mourning for Xerxes in the early stages of his maturation when the drive to overwhelm the parents was the son's goal. There is in an essay of Melanie Klein a description in psychodynamic terms of just this sort of rivalry and its repressive power in blocking the ability to mourn.

> We know the part rivalry plays in the child's burning
> desire to equal the achievements of the grown-ups. In
> addition to rivalry, his wish, mingled with fears, to
> "grow out of" his deficiencies . . . is an incentive to
> achievements of all kinds. . . . A time will come, the
> child phantasies, when he will be strong, tall and grown
> up, powerful, rich, and potent, and father and mother
> will have changed into helpless children, or again, in
> other phantasies, will be very old, weak, poor and re-
> jected. The triumph over the parents in such phantasies,
> through the guilt to which it gives rise, often cripples
> endeavors of all kinds. . . . triumph impedes the work
> of early mourning.[12]

The emphasis here is on the connection between early stages of mourning, necessary as the child separates from the parents, and the later
inability to mourn when the early process has been repressed through
the need to triumph over the parents. Moral maturation depends upon
and follows upon stages of mourning in the years before full adult re-
sponsibilities are undertaken.

The dramatic plot reveals the full effect and realization of failure as it
overwhelms Xerxes, who returns totally crushed; but the conclusion of
the plot exhibits the *god*-man annihilated and the *man* who is able to
mourn, and the evidence of that is Xerxes' leading both chorus and audience in an expression of mourning. An ironic way to connect early
and late stages of mourning is this: the deluge of genuine grief at the
end of the action never would have been necessary if Xerxes had
mourned in his youth; the inability to mourn, then, led with necessity
to the terrible loss of the Persian youth and a final (I say ironic), genuine transformation of the child-god into a mortal adult. *The Persians* is
fully aware of this ironic necessity and uses the psychological reality to
help us understand the historical reality.

In a recent psychoanalytic inquiry into mourning, Hans W. Loewald
remarks that the dynamic propulsion that moves a person through the
stages of maturation, especially that which might be called "moral ma-

---

12. Melanie Klein, "Mourning and Its Relation to Manic-Depressive States," in
Contributions to Psychoanalysis, 1921–1945, ed. Hanna Segal (London: Hogarth
Press, 1948), 319.

turation," is the process of mourning. He writes with a certain technicality, but I think the assertion can be helpful to my discussion of *The Persians*. "The outcome of mourning can show us something like a new intake of objects into the superego structure insofar as elements of the lost object, through the mourning process, become introjected in the form of ego-ideal elements and inner demands and punishments."[13] I believe this description has a *cultural* implication.

The process sketched out by Loewald does have a conceptual connection to both Aristotle's analysis of plot and Freud's analysis of mourning. The dimension added by Loewald is that which I would call "developmental time"; it is the final organizing principle of the tragic drama, to be added to historical time and to plot time.

Tragic actions occur in and make representations of time, yet as they do this they *create* a time of their own as we experience them here and now—*our* dramas, yet a legacy from another culture. Both historical time and plot time are conscious (to greater or less degree) for the artist and for the audience and occupy more or less "objective" positions in the plot and character of the tragic drama. In contrast, developmental time is expressive of unconscious beliefs, wishes, attitudes, and even theoretical assumptions that form the deepest part of the object that we the audience witness from our psychological position as it has been culturally formed in our own moment of historical awareness. Through psychoanalytic theory, access is gained to developmental time. But I do not approach that deep part of the play until I have explored historical time—the Persian attack on Greece, the Greek defense, the Persian loss; and then plot time—the action in which the son, Xerxes, assumes power under the filial trammels of the father, Darius, and the mother, Atossa. The overall interpretation that psychoanalytic theory offers expresses developmental time, the deepest ways in which human beings share in culture—the transhistorical-transfamilial reality we all inherit, live in, and leave to posterity. That time transcends the immediacy of actions such as Greek-Persian warfare and growing up in a specific family, as we see in the case of Xerxes, and looks to the future as a function of both historical-political acts and private conflicts. Thus

13. Hans W. Loewald, "Internalization, Separation, Mourning, and the Superego," in *Papers on Psychoanalysis* (New Haven: Yale University Press, 1980), 257–76.

the conflict that generates tragedy—the conflict between the public and the private—has its *cultural towardness*, that is, it lays down conditions that will come to be realized in a future outside the dramatic time of the play itself. Tragedy itself as an art form develops through the passing of time.

It is that future in cultural evolution I explore in the chapters that follow. Our modern ways with tragedy are the "towardness" of the original tragic dramas—they have a fate as cultural objects, a fate that in a metaphoric sense could be thought of as a future life, a development in and through culture.

III

A psychological future for the dramatic hero occurs as a precondition for the psychological future of the audience, who have been themselves led into the process of mourning. In *The Persians* it may seem that in the play itself there is nothing at the end but mourning, stasis, tears, and moans. But from the audience's point of view, and in the experience of the audience, the dramatic outcome is the ability to mourn and therefore to have a future at all. And that comes about because Xerxes achieves the ability to mourn. Futurity is realized through mourning.

The process through which the audience is led in witnessing an aesthetically well-constructed play like *The Persians* conforms, I believe, to the following description of mourning given by Freud in his essay "Mourning and Melancholia":

> We do not even know the economic means by which mourning carries out its task. Possibly, however, a conjecture will help us here. Each single one of the memories and situations of expectancy which demonstrates the libido's attachment to the lost object is met by the verdict of reality that the object no longer exists; and the ego, confronted as it were with the question whether it shall share this fate, is persuaded by the sum of the narcissistic satisfaction it derives from being alive to sever its attachment to the object that has been abolished. We may perhaps suppose that this work of severance is so slow and gradual that by the time it has

been finished the expenditure of energy necessary for it
is also dissipated.[14]

A similar process is involved in catharsis, though the time of dramatic
presentation can be only a symbol of the long process of mourning that
the audience will have to undergo before the terrible loss is internally
reconciled. Here I can only conjecture upon the intricate ways in which
a cultural object, a play such as *The Persians*, realizes through an aesthetic means a developmental end in everyday life.

The success of *The Persians* as a tragedy derives from its establishment of mourning as a positive, reconstructive act, not simply a
collapse into infantile passivity. That Xerxes truly mourns is given dramatic reality by his solitude, his being alone at the end as a human
being, not a god; without the father, without the mother, and without
the mantle of narcissistic power-trappings with which he was clothed
by his family. Mourning completes the temporal sequence of past-
present-future by creating a future that is a human future—not a future, as in the *Oresteia*, of god-guided community.[15]

Moving from the historical through the developmental to the cultural, we are able to become aware of the plot that drives itself into the
future, for we who witness the drama become mourners as we internalize the dead, just as the characters at the close of the play, Xerxes
and the chorus, perform a ritual mourning that symbolizes the process
of internalization. We are alone with the ghosts of our past, but the
ghosts are now within us. In this perspective Xerxes becomes, oddly,
the hero of the drama in a proper sense, for he internalizes objects that
make a future possible. He has been led through (by the dramatist), or
rather he has exhibited (to the audience), three stages of the development of the hero: early pre-Oedipal passivities, as realized through
Atossa's dream; Oedipal conflicts and competitions with the father, as
realized in the words spoken by the ghost of Darius; and mature post-
Oedipal superego completion of the self through the process of mourn-

14. Freud, "Mourning and Melancholia," in *Std. Ed.*, 14:255.
15. "The establishment of the superego completes the constitution of an inner world
whose dimensions may be said to be the temporal modes past, present, and future"
(Hans W. Loewald, "Superego and Time, in *Papers on Psychoanalysis*, 43–52).

ing that comes upon Xerxes when his inability to mourn is transformed into the ability to mourn.

Being able to mourn brings the fallen Xerxes up out of the grave of fault and witless infatuation—he was responsible for the deaths of the young men of Susa—into a future in which political wisdom may (there is a dreadful doubt here) guide future leaders. Xerxes is transformed; he has realized maturity. The audience may leave the theater in the belief that there *is* a future for the city—but what a terrible tragic reality confronts us: that humankind in their political and sexual lives are doomed to a process of becoming morally mature through being morally corrupt! Yes, we are *doomed* to mourn, and in mourning to create a future out of the infatuations of the past. Futurity comes about through internalization of all the dead who have filled the waters and strewn the land. At the end, in mourning, we may come to understand yoking afresh in all of its political, sexual, psychological, and cultural metaphoric extensions. The metaphor comes clear at least . . . but "at last" is too late. To have a future, we must internalize the most terrible truth: the *at last* that is, for those who mourn, *too late*.

2   Anticipations of Tragedy: Finding and Loss in The Merchant of Venice

Finding is the first Act
The second loss
Third Expedition for
The "Golden Fleece"
Fourth, no Discovery
Fifth no Crew
Finally, no Golden Fleece
Jason—sham—too.

Emily Dickinson

Several of Shakespeare's plays examine tragic conflicts from a distance, as if commenting upon them without subjecting the audience to them. One such "paratragedy"—in the sense of "beside" or "alongside" tragedy—is *The Merchant of Venice*. I shall discuss it in terms of its tragic insights even though it is a drama with—at least on the surface—a happy conclusion. If it is a comedy, it presents a deeply serious inner concern, and I shall begin with the evidence for the central conflict as it presents itself through mythic figures.[1]

The characters in *The Merchant of Venice* move in and out of a mythic place, Portia's home, Belmont. That this place possesses a mysterious ambience in contrast to the commercial realism of Venice was observed by W. H. Auden in his comments on the play: "Without the

1. My reading of the play is dependent upon the recent work of several interpreters. I am indebted to the reading offered by Barbara Tovey in "The Golden Casket: An Interpretation of *The Merchant of Venice*," in *Shakespeare as Political Thinker*, ed. John Alvis and Thomas G. West (Durham, N.C.: Carolina Academic Press, 1981), 215–37; and to the lecture presented by Francis Baudry at the New York Freudian Society, March 4, 1988, entitled, "The Search for Meaning and Significance in *The Merchant of Venice*." I have also benefited from discussions of the play with André Green.

Venice scenes, Belmont would be an Arcadia without any relation to actual times and places, and where, therefore, money and sexual love have no reality of their own, but are symbolic signs for a community in a state of grace."[2] In *The Merchant of Venice* the mysterious beauty we associate with Arcadia is but an aspect of a larger mythic presence. Mythic references surround the figure of Portia:

> Nor is the wide world ignorant of her worth,
> For the four winds blow in from every coast
> Renowned suitors, and her sunny locks
> Hang on her temples like a golden fleece,
> Which makes her seat of Belmont Colchos' strond,
> And many Jasons come in quest of her.

> (1.1)

As we hear these words, we create a scene in which the mythic past of Jason's conquest joins with the love-smitten Bassanio's wish to woo the noble philosophic lady carrying the name of Cato's daughter. One part of that scene remains slightly concealed—that which hides Portia's affinity to Medea, the daughter of Aetes, king of Colchis; the beautiful woman through whose command of black magic Jason was enabled to win the fleece—and the woman. In one of the source stories for *The Merchant of Venice (Il Pecerone)*, the Lady of Belmont is represented as having witchlike powers, though it is never said explicitly that she is a witch. In the *Merchant*, we are led to think of Portia as having close affinity to two male progenitors, Cato and the king of Colchis, and therefore speaking and acting out of a double power. We might think of that power as reason-guided philosophy and passion-driven magic. But we are not encouraged to see Portia in these terms till later in the action; at first we are compelled to see her beauty, her playfulness, and her affinity to the gold of commerce and of physical effulgence.

Golden fleece and golden locks shall reverberate throughout the action in the gold of Venice, the gold of Shylock's treasure, and the gold of the rings given by Portia and Nerissa to their husbands. But even more striking, the gold of fleece and hair returns in the descriptions of

---

2. W. H. Auden, "The Shakespearean City," in *The Dyer's Hand* (New York: Vintage Books, 1968), 234.

Portia herself as Bassanio is tested in choosing among the three caskets.
I shall present those images in a moment; but consider now the figure
of Portia as philosopher-witch. The gold of commerce, of magic, of
fidelity, of wisdom mixes with the gold of mere appearance, deception,
and death. Indeed, Portia's dual potencies command the action in wonderful ways that grant her great powers, though she is trammeled by
her father's condition for her finding a husband. Listen to her description of that legacy:

> . . . the lott'ry of my destiny
> Bars me the right of voluntary choosing:
> But if my father had not scanted me,
> And hedged me by his wit to yield myself
> His wife, who wins me by the means I told you, . . .
>
> (2.1)

Yet Portia wins the man she wants to possess, as Nerissa predicts she
will, for though denied choice, she controls in a mysterious way the
contents of the three caskets. They are themselves mythic objects
standing at the confluence of powerful forces: her father's will; her
own powers, of which we are at first not aware; and the symbolic potencies of the caskets' metals and their enclosed effigies. Their sheer
fixating presence is due not only to their being the way to win the
woman; they elicit strong feelings from each of the contestants (Mo-
rocco, Aragon, Bassanio), whose words express passion. It is the
passionate side of Portia's presence that will demonstrate her powers
beyond those of good sense and philosophical rationality. The mythic
world of Belmont is the realm where the strongest feelings are bred,
feelings powerful enough to meet in deadly combat the passion of Antonio and the passion of Shylock. Ours is a plot of agonistic confron-
tations that call upon both head and heart, both self-preserving and
sexual drives whose organization is derived from commercial Venice
and mythic Belmont.

I shall dwell on the significance of the caskets a bit more. Where
there is wooing there is marriage, where there is marriage there are
children; yet the plot we have within the five acts allows wooing and
marriage without sexual consummation, and suggests children only
most indirectly. It is curious that a condition laid down by Portia's fa-

ther is that those who fail must promise never again to woo (". . . if you choose wrong / Never to speak to lady afterward / In way of marriage . . ." [2.1]). Yet the atmosphere is highly charged sexually, and almost every scene possesses a sexual connotation. This is also true of the caskets. They are cases within which figures or effigies are secreted; that they are female-connected symbols is all too obvious, and we do not need Freud's essay "The Theme of the Three Caskets" to tell us that. The male wooers think sexual thoughts:

> GRA. We'll play with them the first boy for a thousand ducats.
> NER. What! and stake down?
> GRA. No, we shall ne'er win at that sport and stake down.
>
> (3.2)

Thus ends the scene in which Bassanio has won Portia and they have exchanged gold rings. The next "event" must be the "staking down," as Gratiano, who is affianced to Nerissa, lewdly points out.

In fact, the caskets seem more fecund of little folk than either of the couples; in each is a head, though they are of death and madness and only one of lively presence, Portia's portrait. But consider her portrait as it is thought about by Bassanio in making his choice and as it is described once he opens the casket. Follow the golden thread:

> BAS. Look on beauty,
> And you shall see 'tis purchased by the weight,
> Which therein works a miracle in nature,
> Making them lightest that wear most of it:
> So are those crisped snaky golden locks
> Which make such wanton gambols with the wind
> Upon supposed fairness, often known
> To be the dowry of a second head,
> The skull that bred them in the sepulchre.
>
> (3.2)

It is obvious that the associations are to the Medusa head and to the ways in which seeming beauty covers and disguises ugliness, even death. And when Bassanio gazes upon Portia's portrait, these are some of his observations:

BAS. . . . here in her hairs
The painter plays the spider, and hath woven
A golden mesh t'entrap the hearts of men
Faster than gnats in cobwebs. . .

(3.2)

Even in her loveliness there is the golden thread that connects Portia to
Medea, to Medusa, and to the false hair stolen from the sepulchre. We
should then be warned that Portia is no ordinary woman, in any of her
capacities. Having observed her mythic connections, let us move to the
ways in which her golden aspects establish affinities to that other gold,
the gold of commercial, money-lending Venice.

The rich possess gold; they own ducats, as do Antonio and Shylock.
But owners run the risk of robbery or of faithless children who run off
with the family jewels, as does Jessica. We learn that she not only took
two stones from Shylock, her father, but also traded a ring given by her
mother to her father, for a monkey (3.1). Here we have the only suggestion that among the central characters there is any baby making,
but it is a travesty of gestation and birth—a travesty consistent, furthermore, with Jessica and Lorenzo as lovers (5.1) who, sitting in the
moonlight of Belmont, recall all the faithless lovers of the classical past.
Indeed, Jessica's father wishes her "dead at my foot, and the jewels in
her ear: would she were hears'd at my foot, and the ducats in her coffin . . ." (3.1).

The only true pregnancy achieved in the action is that between
Launcelot Gobbo and the female Moor. All else is sterility—of gold,
money lending, usury, sodomy, and the childless couples whose only
"babies" seem to be in coffins.

With such a spectrum of negative sexuality, it is to be expected that
the presence of gold would have yet another implication, that of castration. In English, "gild" and "geld," "gilded" and "gelded" have sometimes interchangeable meanings. The words of the drama bear this out,
for gelding and "marring" are actions imagined and feared. Gratiano
angrily replies to Nerissa on being accused of faithlessly giving away
the ring she had given him:

By yonder moon I swear you do me wrong,
In faith I gave it to the judge's clerk,—
Would he were gelt that had it for my part . . .

. . .

About a hoop of gold, a paltry ring
That she did give me, whose posy was
For all the world like cutler's poetry
Upon a knife, "Love me and leave me not."

(5.1)

And this outburst is followed by:

Well, do you so: let not me take him then,
For if I do I'll mar the young clerk's pen.

(5.1)

Gold, then, has many implications, an expanding aura of connotations that connect it finally to the very denial of fecundity—to sodomy in the case of Antonio, to usury in the case of Shylock, and to castration in the case of Gratiano and Bassanio. So for all its positive connotations of beauty and wisdom, it also hides within it the negative powers of the golden snaky locks whose owner's piercing gaze turns to stone and whose golden gifts are like cutler's poetry, castrating instruments. We never clearly understand Portias power, with all her inbred rationality and passion, to win Bassanio to her bed. Of that much more needs to be said. However, the probability of a happy consummation in a hypothetical sixth act seems dim; and the more we think about the conclusion of this drama, the more it seems to be a comment upon certain themes of tragedy. There is a hopelessness in each of the lovers' efforts at happiness.

I

The Merchant of Venice exhibits affinities to several of Shakespeare's tragedies, each in its own preoccupation a dire intensification of the "problem" in our seeming comedy. Loving couples anticipate babies, as Gratiano says in his challenge to Bassanio; yet all the "babies" represented are in caskets or perverse, as is the monkey Jessica gets in barter for her father's jewels. There is a strange similarity to the theme of childlessness as it occurs in *Macbeth*. In his reading of *Macbeth*, Freud was the first to notice the central importance of childlessness; in his essay "Some Character Types Met with in Psycho-Analytic Work" he discovered the unconscious conflict that underlies Macbeth's manifest "ambition." There is in *Macbeth* a hidden "dead" (that is, unborn) child, as André Green has pointed out to me—not the child Lady Macbeth dashes against the wall in the manic fantasy of her own cruelty brought on by the intention to win the crown, but the fated complexity of the fact that Macbeth cannot have children, has none, and therefore must be totally obliterated by time. Infertility as destiny emerges more and more desperately as the action proceeds. Setting the two plays side by side, we see that the *Merchant*, although a comedic fantasy full of love and coupling, contains, as does *Macbeth*, a hidden presence, which is a hidden absence.

The *Merchant* contains another, much more elaborate and in some respects much more private, allusion to hidden presences. Alluded to, but nowhere explicitly commented upon, is the presence of the author's literary lineage—his predecessors without whom he cannot produce offspring, yet from whom he is declaring his independence in that very drama we witness. There is in *The Merchant of Venice* a set of hidden historical figures in the description of suitors Nerissa and Portia review when we first meet them (1.2). The argument for the suitors' identities has been made by Barbara Tovey and me in an essay that explores Shakespeare's subtle—one might say "latent"—references. Our interpretations identify the Neapolitan Prince as Boccaccio, the County Palatine as Spenser, Monsieur Le Bon as Montaigne, Falconbridge as Chaucer, the Scottish Lord as Henryson, and the Duke of Saxony's nephew as Hans Sachs. But the full significance of the slyly introduced great predecessors remains to be established. All of the hidden writer-suitors are descended from Boccaccio in one way or another, so we think it especially significant that Bassanio was introduced to Portia (1.2) by the Marquis of Montferrat, a character in Boccaccio's *Decameron*.[3]

My thought at this time is that in *The Merchant of Venice* we witness an author cutting himself free from his predecessors, his "parents," much as the characters within the drama are effecting a sep-

3. Richard Kuhns and Barbara Tovey, "Portia's Suitors," *Philosophy and Literature* 13, no. 2 (October 1989): 325–31.

aration from *their* parents. Yet at the same time, both within and without the drama there is a basic acknowledgment that the younger generation receives an endowment from the parents. In the play the endowment is represented not only through the manifest father-daughter inheritances, but also in the latent continuation of the lineage set forth through the oblique descriptions of Portia's suitors. For since the one who introduces Portia and Bassanio to one another is the Marquis of Montferrat, a character in Boccaccio's *Decameron,* and since it is the potent creativity of Boccaccio that ties together all the author-suitors—each has been given a "dower," as it were, from that source of character and plot—the ultimate joining of Bassanio to Portia has a meaning beyond that of a love match. It is also the artist achieving the most intimate commerce with the Muse, embodied in his literary predecessors. We witness the final lovers' match as if it were the culmination of a historical artistic sequence as well as a dramatic stage in Bassanio's love life. The author of the *Merchant* is last in the artistic lineage, and once more myth is related to history: myth has meaning in the "real" world, and reality expresses itself in myth. Thus art represents life, as we say; and we ought to add, life's latent meanings can be exhibited through the artistic use of myth.

Further reflection on this knot of plot and character in history and in the enactment itself leads me to think of the source, *The Decameron,* as that which *The Decameron* describes itself as being: a pimp, a go-between, a Galeot. Boccaccio gave to his book the subtitle of *Principe Galeotto,* Prince Galeot. The reference is clear: the cognomen comes from Dante's *Divine Comedy,* canto 5 of "The Inferno," where in the circle of the lustful the adulterous lovers Paolo and Francesca are confronted by the pilgrim-poet. From Francesca's lips Dante hears the sad tale of the lovers having been brought to illicit love by the agency of a book, a book in which they read of the love of Lancelot and Guinevere, brought together in *their* love by the pander Galahalt.

> Galeotto fu il libro e chi lo scrisse . . .
> (A Galeotto was the book and he who wrote it . . .)

Authors and their books are pimps; so *The Decameron* functions in *The Merchant of Venice,* bringing together Bassanio and Portia.

In that sense Boccaccio vies with Portia's father as the maker of matches.

Portia's suitors, are clear presences, yet hidden. They are necessary "parents" but necessarily to be disowned, as indeed Jessica disowns her father in our play. Shakespeare "disowns" his "fathers" through affectionate contempt, a common way of expressing both love and independence. The drama we witness is Shakespeare's own creation, generated by him alone. In the words of André Green, it is "a child that the writer has brought into the world by himself, without anybody's help, for even though he may be indebted to his precursors, he is its sole creator, the only father—both the father and the mother, for that matter. . . . The writer bypasses any sexual theory involving the parents, since he is at the same time both parents joined for the procreation of the child he has produced."[4]

Belmont, Portia, the childless couples, the "dead" babies alongside the lively quick child that is the unfolding drama itself—all that now takes on a fresh look, as does the power of the heroine both to argue a case in court and to seduce the man she chooses away from his male lover. Portia is the "mother" of this action in several senses that are beginning to emerge. And the denial of choice imposed through her father's "scanting" is succeeded by a deep action of choosing both in the world of commercial-legalistic Venice and in that of fantasy-fairy-land-bewitched Belmont. Portia's powers include the power to change her sex—not surprising in an Elizabethan drama, but now of special importance to *this* action.

Portia has two fathers: Cato, the philosopher from whom she gains her wisdom and power of argument; and Aetes, king of Colchis, from whom she inherits her dark arts of magic and passionate persuasion. There is a further suggested progenitor in Portia's identity as Medea: according to one myth, Medea's mother was Hecate, the goddess who presides over the three ways and is triple-faced; she represents the three aspects of woman as mother, as lover, and as death. Although this seems a heavy burden for the diminutive Portia to bear, the associations were all well known to Shakespeare. The mythic allusions contribute to and help to account for a character whose agency in court and in

4. André Green, *On Private Madness* (London: Hogarth Press, 1986), chap. 14, "The Unbinding Process," 346–47.

castle turns out to be more powerful than her initial passivity would suggest.

Portia's task and purpose is to fulfill her father's wish for her betrothal—though the "wish" is so enacted that Portia *must* comply—and once the correct casket has been chosen by a suitor, she must win the suitor to her bed. Ordinarily one would think the accomplishment rather easy, as it is in the source tale for the *Merchant, Il Pecerone*. But Shakespeare has strewn Portia's path with obstacles. Before the marriage with Bassanio can be consummated, she must settle the affairs with Antonio, both the sexual and the commercial. Here, once again, I see a basic conflict of the sort essential to tragic plots. For tragedy is generated by irreconcilable oppositions between the private and the public, between need and obligation. Portia negotiates just such conflicts in her effort to subdue the passion of Shylock with her own passion of wisdom and mercy. To the courtroom, then, we must go for the critical confrontation; it is in the trial that the political and the psychological reveal their irreconcilability.

II

Shylock names the psychic boundaries and vectors that will bedevil the arguments:

> You'll ask me why I rather choose to have
> A weight of carrion flesh, than to receive
> Three thousand ducats: I'll not answer that!
> But say it is my humour,—is it answer'd?
> . . .
> Some that are mad if they behold a cat!
> And others when the bagpipe sings i'th'nose,
> Cannot contain their urine—for affection
> (Master of passion) sways it to the mood
> Of what it likes or loathes . . .
>
> . . .
> So I can give no reason, nor I will not . . .

(4.1)

Clearly the trial must cope with madness, passion, and the irrational, yet within the context of law and argument. And Shylock insists upon the law! He will have that which the law allows; and in that he is passionately uncontrolled, just as he is in his hatred of Antonio.

In this, Shylock is no stranger to the Shakespearean cast of characters: Lear, Macbeth, and Richard III all are driven by passion. How are the excesses of passion to be countered? In the *Merchant*, it seems to me, the passions are countered by passions. The characters whose passionate natures require this external force to control them are Shylock, Antonio, Bassanio, and—though this may seem strange—Portia. Each has a passion to use as energy and as defense. In the case of Portia, her passionate side is revealed first in her confrontation with Shylock, then in her transformation of Bassanio's own passion.

Portia's appearance in court as a doctor of laws has all the drama of trial as theater, for the trial has an ancient lineage in tragedy. Tragic drama often incorporates trial scenes, as for example in the *Oresteia* and in *Othello;* trial-like occasions excite a sense of inexorability and doom. Though it is humans sitting in judgment, the gods are always hovering in the hidden passageways behind the scene. Before the jury and the hidden gods, there is an advocate; in this case it is Portia, whose theme is mercy, an appropriate plea in the court that brings together the two worlds of Venice and Belmont.

"What is mercy but a compassion in our own hearts of another's misfortunes, urging us as far as our power stretches to relieve him? This *feeling* serves reason, when our pity offends not justice, either in relieving the poor or forgiving the penitent. . . . these *passions* that befall a wise man, so as they do not offer any prejudice to his reason or virtue, are no vices . . ." (emphasis added). So writes St. Augustine in *The City of God,* Book 9, chap. 5. Kierkegaard suggests an added dimension to our thoughts about mercy in his comment on passion: "The highest passion in a man is faith." In the trial scene this can be applied to the protagonists: Shylock's highest passion, and therefore his faith, is the law; Portia's is mercy. Her invoking of mercy calls upon Shylock to allow a competing passion into his breast; for the demands of mercy are, as St. Augustine makes clear, the demands of *feeling,* and a *reasonable* person may properly express—indeed, even be carried away by—such feelings. There is a wonderful passion in God, whose dominant passion is wrath; yet beside that, there is a countervailing passion of mercy. So Portia importunes Shylock: Be subject to that countervailing passion!

We must understand mercy and that which it demands of us, but we have little guidance because moral theory tends to neglect the passion of mercy. We speak more readily of "compassion," of "amnesty," of "generosity," and of "forgiveness." None of these is mercy. What then is mercy?

It seems to me that mercy is a moral passion. One cannot be merciful through reason alone; there must be a strong feeling towards the person and the act, a strong feeling that stands against another strong feeling, so that within the moral consciousness a conflict occurs: a conflict between moral condemnation and the wish to soften, divert, transform that condemnation into a feeling of human companionability. Perhaps the conflict of feelings is an internal anticipation of the public conflict in the courtroom. At the same time, mercy depends upon a clear assessment of the moral values at stake; in the argument between Shylock and Portia these values allow the opportunity for Shylock to receive compensation in money, as originally contracted, so that he can readily give up the harsh demand of the law. Yet Shylock "craves" the law, that is, he has a passion in the grip of which he cannot relent. There is no power of reason in him, only the power of passion— passion on behalf of that which he would call reason, the law. And he is so determined morally that no other passion can be generated in him. His religiosity is such that no countervailing emotion can oppose his craving for the law; analogously, his Christian opponent, Antonio, is so constituted that no countervailing passion can be generated to oppose his homosexuality. Thus, in a deep psychological sense, Antonio's flesh *craves* Shylock's knife.

But what of the passion suffered by Portia? She too is in the grip of a power other than reason, the power of the feeling she calls mercy. She rightly associates it with God and with kings. There is a moral greatness in the capacity to be merciful. For it is not the product of reason, in contrast to acts such as amnesty and forgiveness that may be reasonable responses to argument. What argument can there be for mercy? And does Portia provide one?

Portia argues that mercy's seat is with God and in the hearts of kings, above the scepter of temporal power; it is a gift from realms above, and simply enters the earthly realm as a "gentle rain from heaven." Thus it is an endowment not born in us, but striking a responsive chord in us if we are so attuned. What then are the conditions that predispose us to mercy? Here there is no direct answer, but an indirect one is hidden in the language of the play.

There is not one character in the drama who exhibits merciful conduct towards another, save Portia towards Bassanio. A brief survey of others' behavior demonstrates a lack of that passion we are pursuing. For example, Launcelot Gobbo treats his father cruelly, misleading the father about the son's death; Antonio plays upon Bassanio's feelings of guilt and promotes his own feelings of having been mistreated; Jessica is mean to her father; and Shylock expresses nothing but anger towards his daughter. Where then is mercy in the plot? Certainly the Duke and the Magnificoes of Venice urge Shylock to be merciful, but they themselves are not. Where is mercy in this drama? It seems to me that there is only one merciful action; that is when Portia accepts Bassanio as he is, to be her husband, since she knows that his passion is directed towards Antonio. But mercy instructs her to be passionately winning, that is, to use her deepest feelings to overcome Bassanio's passion. Here there is a truly merciful action, but not one that is evident on the surface.

After the trial, both Bassanio and Gratiano give away their marriage pledges to those they take to be men; both Portia and Nerissa must counter their husbands' dereliction, their violation of the bond, analogous to the bond between Shylock and Antonio. If the women insisted upon the law, they would be justified in breaking off the marriages, neither consummated. Yet they are passionately in love, and another passion coexists with love: mercy. Passion directs action. We enter here into the passionate foundation of the actions in this play, in which the combat of the passions leads to resolution.

Passion is a function of the body, and this play emphasizes the body in several striking ways. The first, of course, is the pledge, a pound of flesh. In the trial scene the physicality of the contract—the cutting, weighing, and bloodletting of the flesh—is forced upon us. Second, Shylock seems to be obsessional about bodies. For example:

> If I can catch him once upon the hip,
> I will feed fat the ancient grudge I bear him.

(1.3)

> Hear you me Jessica,
> Lock up my doors, and when you hear the drum
> And the vile squealing of the wry-neck'd fife
> Clamber not you up to the casements then
> Nor thrust your head into the public street
> To gaze on Christian fools with varnish'd faces:
> But stop my house's ears, I mean my casements,
> Let not the sound of shallow fopp'ry enter
> My sober house.

(2.5)

We ought also to remember the parable of Jacob's sheep, told by Shylock (1.3). The "work of generation" produces more fat bodies to fill the usurer's bins.

Shylock's helplessness in the grip of his passions ought not surprise us, then, if we see the extent to which he is rooted in the body. Is it the fate of Judaism to be so rooted? Perhaps; but then we are shown a like bodily rootedness in Christian behavior. The central Christian exhibit here is that of Antonio and Bassanio in their friendship: there has been unhealthy indulgence on the one side and opportunistic exploitation of that indulgence on the other. They are in the grip of sexual passion, rooted in the body, but their passion can be extirpated only by a countervailing passion, as a kind of conversion. Shylock's passion also can be removed only through "conversion."

Thus there are two sorts of conversion going on: that from Judaism to Christianity; and that from homosexual attachment to heterosexual attachment. I shall follow the two paths of conversion.

Shylock's helplessness in the grip of passion, his inability to entertain an alternative to his demand for justice according to the letter of the contract, ought not surprise us when we understand the extent to which he is what he is as a *bodily* self.

The Merchant of Venice suggests in its representation of the Jew, Shylock, that Judaism imposes a bodily fate upon the Jew. There is little doubt that in this play ritual circumcision as a condition for being that which is of Judaism arouses in the Christian feelings both moral and genital. Morally, the Christian is called upon to repress the representation of a genital wound in order to sustain legal fairness (especially in a court of law). There is a fantasy presence in the court: the imaginative presence of mutilation in that part of the body around which contradictory feelings cluster. The drama proposes the possibility that Judaism is a bodily religion through its representative, Shylock, whose language dwells continually upon the body. But is this characteristic peculiar to Judaism? The drama suggests it is, but only until the implications of Christianity are subtly set out in its representatives, Antonio and Bassanio. Their friendship rests upon the grip of sexual passion rooted in the body.

My analysis has arrived at a basic conflict in the drama, a conflict generated by bodily states and ideological aspirations in their political incompatibilities. I shall discuss the deepest levels of this conflict in terms of two concepts, that of the bodily ego and that of conversion. "Bodily ego" is a psychoanalytic concept; "conversion" is meaningful in three areas—those of logic, of religion, and of the law.

As the theory of ego development was expanded and refined in the course of psychoanalytic reflections upon the making of the self, it became obvious to Freud that the first and most basic stage of ego development is that which he called a "bodily ego." He wrote in *The Ego and the Id:* "The ego is first and foremost a bodily ego; it is not merely a surface entity, but is itself the projection of a surface." In a footnote added later, he wrote: "I.e. the ego is ultimately derived from bodily sensations, chiefly those springing from the surface of the body. It may thus be regarded as a mental projection of the surface of the body, besides, as we have seen above, representing the superficies of the mental apparatus."[5] The psychoanalytic formulation provides insight into Shylock's character and the source of some of his actions and assertions.

As the ego develops throughout life, it not only gathers into itself external objects and persons, but forms itself in and through body feelings, body contacts, and the body configuration of the person; all these

5. Freud, *The Ego and The Id,* in *Std. Ed.,* 19:26.

aspects are internalized as irremovable dynamic elements in the psychic apparatus. Shylock, in the setting of a Christian polity, has internalized a bodily ego that represents the ways in which Shylock is regarded by the others, that is, the Christian others. His basic bodily ego begins with a disfiguration, and that internal wound is expressed in the contract Shylock proposes. Thus Shylock's passion for justice is rooted in the body, the bodily ego, which sees itself as forever subservient to *its* contract—its religion, from which conversion is impossible. No Jew can "become" a Christian, in part because there is the physical dedication to Judaism symbolized by circumcision. Yet Portia undertakes to lead Shylock to conversion through pleading with him to show mercy to the one he "has upon the hip." Thus we can see Portia's request for mercy as having a definite meaning to Shylock: it is a first move in a translation that ultimately would lead to a Jew becoming a Christian. Mercy itself is a passion that must work as a countervailing passion to Shylock's passion for the law. Reason cannot arouse a countervailing passion where the bodily ego has internalized a Christian community's view of Judaism. And to a Jew, to hold together the passions of wrath and mercy would lead the Jew into the most dangerous imitation, namely, the imitation of God, for whom those two passions are forever in conflict.

The Merchant of Venice explores all the meanings and implications of "conversion." In two cases, Portia must be the agent of conversion: first, in bringing Shylock into the Christian fold by demanding mercy from him; second, in bringing Bassanio into the heterosexual fold by enabling him to be her lover. Each case calls upon a different side of her character. To convert Shylock, Portia the "daughter" of Cato exercises her philosophic power in an effort to counter Shylock's passion for justice with the hoped-for passion of mercy. However, philosophical argument does not in itself guarantee a passionate response, and in the end reason must fail.

In the case of Bassanio, the conflict is of a different sort, sexual rather than religious. Here the "conversion" Bassanio stands in need of is moving from his past homosexual attachment to Antonio to his future heterosexual attachment to Portia. To effect this conversion, Portia must rely upon her powers as a witch, her Medea inheritance. Only as a golden-haired sorceress can she win Bassanio to her bed.

The Merchant of Venice refers to conversion in three domains of thought and action. The first domain we become aware of in the drama is logic; here subjects and predicates are "converted" in such inferences as, No Jews are Christians; therefore no Christians are Jews. As he considers running from Jew to Christian, Launcelot Gobbo performs several conversions in thought and utterance. His ruminations are full of specious reasonings and efforts at logical conversions by which he might justify his running away from Shylock. His irrelevant uses of "ergo" suggest this:

> But I pray you ergo old man, ergo I beseech you,
> talk you of young Master Launcelot.
>
> (2.2)

Launcelot's "arguments" are full of linguistic mistakes; the purpose of the florid malapropisms is to rationalize the breaking of an obligation. Launcelot's "conversion" from Jew to Christian is based upon logical conversions and has little to do with belief.

The second domain in which the idea of conversion appears is religion. Religious conversion implies a shift in basic belief, preceded usually by a deep emotional experience. We can hardly expect Portia's description of mercy to lift Shylock out of one passion into another, i.e., out of one religion into another, since that is what it would mean to Shylock were he to take the first step.

There is a third, unfamiliar sense of "conversion": a legal sense that has to do with misuse of property, either through unlawful appropriation or through unlawful use of property lawfully appropriated. It is in this metaphorically extended sense that I shall understand Portia's task in converting Bassanio, for in a deep sense Bassanio has misused his body, his most intimate and his *own* property, through an alliance with Antonio. While his body is his to do with as he wills, the religious belief underlying the legal sense of conversion includes beliefs about the body, God's own created object whose uses are subordinate to God's will. Where the body's sexuality is concerned, proper and improper sexual uses come into view. Bassanio's legal conversion must correct the misuse of his property, his body, which he has converted once in the legal sense and which now stands to be converted back again in a sexual sense. Portia as philosopher and witch must raise the appropriate passion in her would-be lover; she succeeds with Bassanio, though she has failed with Shylock. Is the conversion of Bassanio the successful result of the force of mercy?

Though there is talk of mercy in the court, little mercy is shown to anyone at all, as I have pointed out. Portia's noble words hang in the air with little effect. It may be that in the end, the one who utters those words is the one most deeply and appropriately affected by those words. It is Portia who must allow the passion of mercy to rise in her breast, and it is towards Bassanio that mercy must be extended.

In the concluding scene, in which the golden rings change hands, we are given the opportunity to see Portia in her most dramatic exercise of passion. She poses her force of magical transforming power against that of the physical Antonio, whose "fat" presence has been amply explored by the poised knife of Shylock. Portia's last analysis of her lover's condition is this:

> In both my eyes he doubly sees himself:
> In each eye one,—swear by your double self,
> And there's an oath of credit.

> (5.1)

And hear that now alongside the words spoken by Bassanio upon seeing Portia's portrait:

> . . . move these eyes?
> Or whether (riding on the balls of mine)
> Seem they in motion? . . .
> . . .
> . . . but her eyes!
> How could he see to do them? having made one,
> Methinks it should have power to steal both his
> And leave itself unfurnish'd . . .

> (3.2)

Bassanio has remarked Portia's powerful eyes that steal away his sense of self; when she herself remarks her eyes, she knows that what he sees is his androgynous person, in each eye one. Thus she must accept that he "swear by [his] double self," for that is the best she can obtain as an "oath of credit." Bassanio's conversion follows taking an "oath of credit" in both the legal and the sexual sense. He "converts" his body from Antonio to Portia, and by being able to commit his body to the woman, he thus restores the property he misused. But it is *she* who wrought the conversion. Will it be binding? We never will know, but doubts are certainly in order. This "oath of credit" matches that of Antonio, who also swore to pay back his debt. Antonio did and did not honor his oath. So, too, Bassanio: he is Portia's husband—and perhaps he is not. But whether he honors and protects her "ring" depends upon the passions the body generates. Reason here is helpless.

Mercy is a moral passion. It turns out to be *the* moral passion under whose sway all passions must be placed, for mercy essentially endows the moral agent with the flexibility to avoid being totally ruined by passion. Even God, whose wrath is tempered by mercy, through the passion of mercy restrains his power to destroy humankind and all its blasphemous aggressions. The ways in which wrath and mercy may subdue one another are a lesson reason may learn and reason may teach. It is a philosophical, not a religious teaching; it is an understanding powerless to raise a feeling.

III

Portia's active participation in the trial and her explication of her passion-driven decision fit well with her choice of Bassanio and the means whereby she initially drew him to herself. It is obvious that she is not in a strategic sense truthful; that is, she dissembles when she needs to win a position. The first such case is right after Bassanio has chosen the leaden casket. She tells him she is "an unlesson'd girl, unschool'd, unpracticed" (3.2). Of course, she is anything but that; and when she subjects herself to Bassanio, taking him as her lord and master, we know there is necessarily magic in the act as well as flattery. Her husband will be brought close to her in these two ways, for he must have certain beliefs about her if he is to be a proper mate.

In short, Portia is transformed from a trammeled, confined, father-directed daughter to a free, powerful woman quite capable of choosing. Yet she was always that; so we wonder why her father saw such limits in her competence.

We are given, through Bassanio's description of the portrait he finds in the leaden casket, a good account of Portia's character and her seemingly passive, then active, ways:

. . . here in her hairs
The painter plays the spider, and hath woven
A golden mesh t'entrap the hearts of men
Faster than gnats in cobwebs . . .

(3.2)

She has been quietly waiting for her prey, spiderlike; and once he is in the net, she becomes aggressive, active, domineering, though with the greatest subtlety.

Under her father's will she was obedient, patient, and watchful. Once the "gnat" is entrapped, she shows her power to choose and to create arguments out of passion, as we see her do in the trial; and she shows her willfulness in how she spins Bassanio in the web of her will when she confronts him with the lost ring. She is mistress of her will, mistress of choice; yet she presides over a "crossroads" where the goddess Hecate dwells. That place is the three-way choosing place of the caskets, and they themselves the symbols of one of Medea's forebears, the Hecate of the three faces. In each casket is a face, and each face explicates a fate that each one of us has: the face of death, of foolishness, and of a fantasied life-companion. We choose our life-companion, and at the same time we are made poignantly aware of foolishness and death. The *other*, the complement to ourself, is chosen at the place where three roads meet; that juncture metaphorically brings together aspects of free, deliberative choice, as well as determined, bound causality. Thus in Bassanio's "choosing" of Portia there is a coercion, as there is in Portia's execution of her father's will. She is at once the goddess Hecate and the protagonist whose range of choice is severely structured by external force. In this respect Portia directs the dramatic plot towards tragedy without its becoming tragic in the dire sense; it is, once more, a view beside tragedy, a "paratragedy," a comment upon tragedy without being an example of it. Tragic choice becomes the deepest subject of this comedy, but it is choice shifted from fate to passion, from an external impersonal force to an internal expression of will and wish.

By what force is choice limited, trammeled, confined? By the force of others' and one's own passion, or by madness as a force within the person. *The Merchant of Venice* is a drama that presents to our watching delight a scene of passions in conflict: Antonio, Shylock, Bassanio, Portia, Jessica, Launcelot Gobbo—all are in the grip of passions they cannot subdue. Just as Portia's father imposed his willful wish upon his daughter, so each character imposes a willful force of passion upon another. Within the person resides an extraordinary urgency to *express*, along with an instrument of direction, like a lens that concentrates the rays of the sun upon one spot.

One escapes this force and its instrument of aim: the poet, Shakespeare, who in rejecting the five poet predecessors frees himself from the willful legacy of having to choose within the parameters they had set. He will be free as no character within the play is free, and certainly free far beyond any freedom granted the tragic hero. He is the poet who does not hear the voice of Hecate, since the poet creates the universe within which passions confine choice. Thus he has constructed the fairy-tale world of Belmont as one to which the character Bassanio comes, led by a character from Boccaccio's *Decameron*. It may be Portia's father who defines the casket choosing, but it is Shakespeare who intervenes to determine how the woman and the man will be paired. To that extent he relies upon the one "father" from whom he could not totally separate himself.

IV

In my analysis of tragedy to be presented in chapter 3, I will separate out three basic elements of plot and character that, it seems to me, are essential to the genre. They are the riddle, psychosexual-political conflict, and splitting. In the *Merchant* we have examined the scene in which the psychosexual-political conflict is most clearly exhibited, the trial. Riddle and splitting remain to be pointed out.

In tragedy riddles are often essential to the plot; the most obvious case is Sophocles' *Oedipus the King* In paratragedy riddles remain subordinate to the business of resolutions in marriage, to intimations of recovery and wholeness (for example, in *The Winter's Tale*). Riddles are often propounded by witches, as in *Macbeth*, so it should not surprise us to find riddles surrounding Portia; the riddle central to the whole plot of the *Merchant* is sounded in the first lines spoken by Antonio ("In sooth I know not why I am so sad . . ." [1.1]) and by Portia

55

("By my troth Nerissa, my little body is aweary of this great world" [1.2]).

Sounding the note of melancholia poses a riddle: Why are the two figures thus beset by sadness and weariness? The play will tell it all, not in an obvious, explicit way, but in an obscure, indirect, partially repressed way. The answer I have pointed to is this: Antonio's sadness results from his anticipation of losing his male lover to a rival, Portia. Further losses are anticipated in Antonio's having *no place* to be housed, to be paired. Portia's weariness results from her seemingly hopeless task to find a mate; she to find, Antonio to lose. Her gain is his loss, but her gain has been shown to be problematic, and one can conjecture that in her philosophical wisdom she knows the burden that falls upon a woman who seeks a mate fitted to both her physical needs and her intellectual powers.

Since Portia has a passionate inner force at the service of her magical powers, she commands situations that to lesser beings pose riddles. The three caskets in themselves are three riddles, to be "solved" by the mind and body equipped to penetrate their mystery. That Bassanio succeeds implies his fitness; yet he is, in respects that puzzle us, a bit weak, a subject to Antonio as he is a subject to Portia. Bassanio is no Oedipus, yet like Oedipus he is terribly unknowing where he ought to be knowing. But as we watch Oedipus *we know* he in some inner sense knows; as we watch Bassanio we see a man surprisingly insensitive to those repressions that must be within a husband who has not made love to a woman. Hence there is a deep riddle within the person of Bassanio, a riddle we shall never clarify. So like tragedy, our paratragedy poses riddles aplenty, but leaves some of them unresolved.

Finally, the *Merchant* cleverly and forcefully provides a commentary upon the tragic necessity of splitting. Not only are there mirrors of characters reflecting characters; there are pairs whose relationships represent splitting in the psychoanalytic sense. Most interesting in this aspect of the play are the figures of Old Gobbo and his son, Launcelot Gobbo. I take the name "Gobbo" to be an echo of the term "gobbet," a lump or mass of flesh, and therefore a reminder of the pound of flesh and the assault on the body that is the central metaphor in the drama. Father and son stand in the relationship of blind, old, weak, maudlin parent to crafty, exploitative, cruel son. But both are split in themselves between Judaism and Christianity, into whose services they enter as opportunists, insofar as their lowly capacities permit. When we meet Launcelot, we find him torn between "fiend" and "conscience," fiend saying, "Budge!" and conscience saying "Budge not!" Conscience says stay with the Jew in the Jew's service; fiend says flee to serve the Christian (2.2). His running away casts him into the presence of his "sand-blind" father, who knows him not. And Launcelot must split his interpretation of religion and family into an affirmation of two contradictory "realities": Judaism and Christianity, and real and fantasy fathers. Just as the name Oedipus has two meanings ("knowing-foot" and "swollen-foot"), so in the *Merchant* names carry two meanings. "Portia" refers at once to the philosopher and the witch; and "Launcelot" refers to the figure who in romance was without known parents (hence the comic line uttered by young Gobbo about old Gobbo, "It is a wise father that knows his own child") and who was a source for the romantic notion that between married couples there can be no love. Love between unmarried lovers comes in sudden passion that leads to adultery. Of course, there is no name in the *Merchant* that has an inner duality, as does the name Oedipus, but there are dualities of reference in the play, derived from the wittily hidden identities of the five suitors, who are at once named (as "Neapolitan Prince") and yet unnamed. We discover the other name. So with Portia and Launcelot; we discover the hidden references.

In the above respects the *Merchant* contains all the elements—psychosexual-political conflict, riddle, and splitting—necessary for tragedy, without, as it were, giving way to tragedy. The action ends with contradictions and splittings resolved; no more are there puzzling instabilities of faith, for as Antonio asserts:

> I once did lend my body for his wealth,
> Which but for him that had your husband's ring
> Had quite miscarried. I dare be bound again,
> My soul upon the forfeit, that your Lord
> Will never more break faith advisedly.
>
> (5.1)

In tragedy faith has been broken prior to the represented action in a deep violation that is both cosmic and moral; hence in tragedy there is no reparation possible. In paratragedy the possibility of there being a "forfeit" in reparation of broken faith seems real, insofar as the action fools itself about itself; but we the watchers know—or suspect—that the forfeit can easily be a vain and hopeless gesture, as indeed it almost was in the case of Antonio.

3   An Intervening Discussion:
     Why We Find Tragic
     Representations Pleasurable

When Freud was fifty years old he was honored by his col-
leagues with the presentation of a medallion on which was engraved
Oedipus confronting the Sphinx; on the reverse was Freud himself,
looking severe and without affect in the traditional profile we associate
with commemorative medals. However he presented himself on the
medallion, he was in fact filled with intense feeling on the occasion of
the presentation; indeed, he was visibly moved—even shaken—by the
inscription on the medal, a quotation from Sophocles' *Oedipus the
King:* "He who answered (as if through divination) the famous riddle
and was indeed a most mighty man." It is tiresome and repetitive to
link Freud with Oedipus, for we forget that Oedipus was not Freud's
invention, but an inherited hero whose exploits and sufferings go far
beyond the event Freud "borrowed" as his clinical metaphor. Yet the
private significance of the link is well expressed by the medal presented
to Freud, for it states that which Freud thought about *himself:* that he
was the solver of a riddle, the deepest that was ever put to humankind,
by humankind, and that his solution was the inevitable outcome of genius that had foreseen its destiny, since Freud had marked that very
sentence from the tragic drama *Oedipus the King* when he was a gym-
nasium student. That in itself is perhaps an Oedipean fate that Freud
was able to appreciate: to know one's destiny, to have it, as it were,
before oneself from early in life is a Greek theme; and it is a reality in
the life histories of many deeply creative individuals.

    For each one of us, destiny shrouds itself in dim futures, and if it
manifests itself to us—as it does dramatically to tragic heroes—the
hint more often than not is hidden in a riddle to be "solved." Thus to
the audience the tragic riddle represents a private mystery surrounded
by a feeling of unfulfilled expectation, as the riddle refers explicitly to

the character whose choices make the plot—and the plot, in its unfold-ing, unriddles the riddle. The special fact about riddles in tragedy is that they are keys to deep insights, that they lead us down into primary-process thought and into the *latent* content of human action. We must *solve* the riddle because when we do, we gain a pathway to the latent, and there is then a way to travel from the latent to the manifest content and back again. With the right interpretative strategy, we can solve the riddle. Lacking the right strategy, we are forever locked out from understanding.

While tragic plots contain directions to the solution of riddles they propound, we who watch may be incapacitated by the contradiction of tragedy: solving the riddle is pleasurable, yet tragedy is full of pain and suffering. Overwhelmed by heroic bafflement, we may overlook the continuity between tragic riddles and our own childhood joy in posing and answering the often-slight and sometimes-silly riddles that every culture delights in. Anthropologists have often pointed out that riddles are expressions of a deep insight: the natural world and the cultural world exhibit remarkable analogies that can be expressed in riddles; and tragic riddles certainly manifest this awareness.

Yet tragedy as the locus of deep riddles still puzzles us, even when we solve the riddles, because it is an art form filled with the most dire suf-ferings, representing the most *painful* of human contradictions and violent actions—yet as art it gives us *pleasure*. How is that possible? Why do we positively *enjoy* watching people chop up one another, per-form perfidious acts upon one another, discover in one another the most horrendous wickedness? Great thinkers from Plato through Tolstoy—and along the way we can count St. Augustine and many straitlaced types—found tragedy not only unbearable, but an ex-pression of human depravity that we ought not witness. And yet, as we all know, nothing is more bracing than a heap of bodies, a plentiful spreading about of pig's blood, and a howling protagonist.

A variety of explanations have been given down through the ages to account for the delight we mortals take in depictions of our sufferings. There is always a philosopher hanging about the entrance to the theater with a model of the human psyche to explain our perversity. Plato ar-gues that going to the tragic theater is like looking at dead bodies outside the city walls: one part of us says, "Don't look," and another part of us says, "Just a peek!" And then at the other gate (assuming the theatrical setting is large, as at Epidaurus) is the other philosopher, in this case Aristotle, who seeks to refute Plato by an argument, as in the *Poetics*, that the peculiar pleasure of the response to the dramatic representation of the painful can be analyzed, for there is a pleasure *appropriate* to tragedy. Here's the rub: "appropriate" means the right pleasure in the right place at the right time, which I assume means I must not snicker when Hamlet falls; must not giggle at Lear's appearance with Cordelia in his arms. But when do I get the pleasure? So let us ask, What is the source of the coextensive pain-pleasure response to tragic action in tragic drama?

Serious scenes of suffering present three elements or conditions that contribute to, though do not exhaust, the complex pain-pleasure response to tragedy. They are (1) a riddle; (2) psychosexual conflict within a political setting; and (3) splitting, a term long used in psychoanalytic theory, first by Freud, and then refined and developed by several of Freud's followers.

A Riddle and Its Strangeness

The most famous riddle in the West is that put to Oedipus by the Sphinx, a riddle Oedipus believes he has satisfactorily answered.[1] Of course the riddle has an answer, which in the play is "Oedipus"— he himself is the riddle, the riddle to which he finds the solution too late. Had Oedipus *understood* the riddle, he would have seen more deeply into his own predicament. To the audience—we who watch— witnessing Oedipus' wrongheadedness, the riddle has a deeper latent meaning he seems to scant—its strangeness. There is a quality in the riddle itself that strikes us as spooky, uncanny. There crouches the bird-beast-woman who propounds riddles about *us*. Why? What business is it of hers that we toddle, stride, and hobble in the stages of our

1. The riddle goes in one version, "What is the creature with one voice which has two, three and four legs?" Answer: man, or humankind. In the ages of our lives we are a child on four, an adult on two, and an aged person leaning on a stick, therefore three. The riddle has a solution, in the formal sense, but in the context of the life of Oedipus the answer is "Oedipus" who is himself the riddle, the riddle Oedipus never answers, namely, "Who am I?" The Sophoclean text is filled with riddles, not the least of which is the very name of Oedipus, which has two meanings: "swollen-foot," and "knowing-foot" or "knowing-way." Which is his name? Are both his name? I will return to this question later.

lives? And should we accept the challenge, and answer correctly, we must witness the horrifying destruction of the importunate lady-beast; should we fail, we satisfy her dire wants. It seems to me that the riddle of the Sphinx—propounded by the feline-woman to the ambitious youth—possesses an element of comic wit, for wit has, in this case as in so many others, a penalty—for Oedipus a severe penalty—attached to failure.

Let us think about the riddle, a common topos in the tradition of story, folktale, novel, and of course detective story. By "topos" I mean a recurring crux, a pattern, a rhetorical occasion for complex meaning. A riddle in the story often provides a model for the larger story of which it is a part; and if we can read the riddle rightly, we may find our way through to the deeper meaning, to the latent and often unconscious level of the thought. When we consider the Oedipean riddle—in another version, "What goes on four in the morning, two at noon, and three in the evening?"—we watchers can test the belief Oedipus so boastfully holds—that he has solved the riddle—by experiencing the drama: the very action of Oedipus in the drama is a playing out of the riddle, with his unawareness of this congruence everywhere obvious. In some sense we *know* the answer, even though we go along with the protagonist as he tries to solve the riddle; part of the excruciating tension in the opening of the tragedy has to do with this stage of *tragic irony*: that we know and he doesn't. But the way we know is strange, wonderful, and uncanny; we know through knowing the very name "Oedipus," yet he who carries the name does not know! In the drama the protagonist's stages of life are clearly set forth: the baby, exposed on the hillside (four); the powerful king (two); and the exiled, cast-out, polluted man, blindly tapping his way towards death (three).

Oedipus is the man with the swollen foot (*oidos*); his name says so. His name also refers to the exposure as an infant, the early wound of pierced ankles; and it has a definite sexual suggestion, the swollen member. Oedipus is the man who knows (*oida*); his name says so, and through knowledge (answering the Sphinx) he gains the throne of Thebes. He is all knower and all ignorant. He boasts he knows; he does not know, even through his own name, who he is, and the meaning of his name seems to be hidden from him.

Oedipus is the foot, the *pous:* the foot that walks, flees, carries him from his birth to his destiny. Oedipus crushes opposition (as with his foot) and is trapped by fate—caught by the foot, as it were. He wanders; he hears stories about his past, but he does not know if they are true; he does not know who his parents are, though he believes he knows; and then he comes to Thebes and shows that he knows who is *dipous, tripous,* and *tetrapous.* Swollen-foot knows all about feet—except about his own. Oedipus moves from king-ruler-judge-knower to defiled person who must leave the city; and his defilement is symbolically his swollen foot. Oedipus is both the highest and the lowest; that is the nature of humankind. The answer to the riddle seems so open, obvious, manifest; yet it is so deep, hidden, latent. Watching the play, we bring the two levels together.

Oedipus is king and *pharmakos* (scapegoat), political leader and the polluted scapegoat who is driven out into the wilderness with the pollutions of the community upon him. This unfathomable coming together of opposites in one person is a riddle.

There is, as I have said, a suppressed comic side to the deepest tragedy, for riddles are kin to jokes; and there is something of a joke in the compilation of opposites in Oedipus. The affinity between jokes and riddles was noted by Freud in his book *Jokes and Their Relation to the Unconscious.* It is an inverse relationship. Jokes reveal and exhibit; riddles conceal and hide. In a riddle we must solve a problem; in a joke a problem is solved for us. Jokes make us laugh; riddles leave us bemused and with a sense of puzzlement. Yet riddles have a touching, often childlike quality, and they often solicit answers that never really fit the question.

Hearing the Oedipus riddle, we find it is something that might be a schoolchild's question, with a simple answer, and yet not really a simple answer. We all know such riddles; they are found in every culture and in every age. Here is an Anglo-Saxon riddle from the *Exeter Book* (seventh to eighth century A.D.):

> Me in those days my father and my mother
> Gave up as dead: I had as yet no life,
> No spirit. Then a loyal kinswoman
> Wrapped me in clothes and kept and cherished me,

Enfolded me in a protective cloak,
As kindly as she did for her own children,
Until, as was my nature, in her care
I became mighty-hearted among those
Who were no kin of mine. Yet my protectress
Still nourished me till I grew up and might
More widely travel. She by doing that
Had less dear sons and daughters of her own.[2]

The answer, "cuckoo" (the bird), seems a simple conclusion to such a rich description, but riddles are like that: it is in the posing of them that we find the deepest thought. The saying of the riddle is often a story, but the answer is out of proportion to the question, sometimes, as in the answer to the Sphinx, it is just one word.

Riddles lie deep in tragedy; we need simply remind ourselves of the dramas we are perhaps more familiar with, those of Shakespeare: *Hamlet, Macbeth,* and *King Lear* all have riddles at their depths. How can the dead Hamlet appear as if in life? Where is Macbeth's vulnerability, told to him in riddles by the three witches? How can the least loving daughter be yet the most loving daughter? What is meant by the riddle spoken by Edgar on the heath, in Lear's presence: "Nero is an angler in the lake of darkness"?

Clever renovations of the riddle in tragedy have been realized by writers of modernity who see through the riddle to its sinister, yet slightly comic, mixture of affects; the most interesting of these modern writers is Heinrich von Kleist, and I shall draw your attention to one of his greatest stories, *Michael Kohlhaas,* in chapter 5. Written about 1808, *Kohlhaas* bears a disturbing likeness to the tradition of tragedy, yet in itself is not a tragedy—not in any obvious sense, but the affects it generates are so complex and unusual that one may declare it is truly tragic. Indeed, there is a riddle—several riddles—at its heart. The story is really about justice, but there are such forceful themes of uncanny presences in the story that it makes justice seem strange, an intervention from another world. The story poses two riddles, at least two: one that is spoken, but to which no solution is given. However, the hero,

2. *A Choice of Anglo-Saxon Verse,* trans. Richard Hamer (London: Faber and Faber, 1970), 99.

Kohlhaas, knows the answer because it has been given to him by a mysterious Gypsy woman; the solution is written on paper, and Kohlhaas swallows it after reading it. We shall never know the answer, a satiric rebuke to classical tragedy with its more obvious riddles. The second riddle has to do with the Gypsy woman who is also the reincarnation of Kohlhaas's dead wife, Lisbeth. And here we encounter in its more anxiety-arousing form a necessary element in the force of tragedy that yields pleasure: the uncanny.

Tragedy always has an element in it of the uncanny. The anxiety provoked by strangeness in the uncanny, and the generation of strangeness out of riddles, test us (the audience) as the protagonist is tested. We are put to the test by the *plot* to see if we are wanting as an audience. But how might we be wanting? What would show us up to the mark, adequate to the role of "good audience?" It is the level at which we can see through to the truth of tragedy, without succumbing to its manifest diversions, that measures us. The term Aristotle uses is "philosophical"; he argues that poetry is more *philosophical* than history, and it is the riddle that first sets us upon the philosophical quest as witnesses of tragedy. And it is the riddle that leads us to an intellectual quest as it generates affect; the riddle helps to control affect because it poses a problem to be solved.

Even in this brief survey of riddles, a few conclusions can be drawn. (1) Tragic riddles set us on a quest, rather like the quest of the protagonist; for they concern the nature of human being and all the mysteriousness about ourselves that we never fully comprehend. Because the riddle is in some respects never satisfactorily solved, it stands as a metaphor for tragedy itself, which is never resolved, never happily concluded—nor really ever concluded at all. (2) Riddles appear in tragedy as if an inevitable component of tragedy; they contribute to the force of plot events as *necessary* in their unfolding because they direct attention to secrets hidden inside the action. Where there are secrets we are driven to unknotting, as if the secret lies inside a tangle to be untangled; and that urgency aroused in us reinforces the urgency of the plot. (3) In offering the riddle, tragedy provides a manifest and a latent meaning to the riddle; the latent is deep, hard to formulate, and resides in the tragedy as a whole. It is like the unconscious; indeed, it may be correct to call the latent meaning of the riddle the unconscious primary-process thought of the drama. (4) Riddles begin in childhood play and accompany us through life, just as the protagonist carries the riddle through life. (5) Finally, riddles are transitional objects functioning on the communal cultural level (analogous to teddy bears and blankets, which also have mysterious powers) and are the objects that introduce us to the uncanny. This is not to say the riddle induces unalloyed pleasure; rather, like everything in tragedy, riddles are pleasures in the painful.

Psychosexual Conflict in a Political Context

The second source of the peculiar pleasure we derive from tragedy comes from, or is a function of, the basic—and I believe the definitional—condition that generates tragedy. It is a psychosexual conflict whose source is the inevitable incompatibility between *private need* and *public obligation*. The most obvious example is, again, that amazing exemplar of the tragic, *Oedipus the King*, and the protagonist of that drama, Oedipus. In all tragic plots, the story gains inextinguishable energy and force from an unresolvable conflict, unresolvable because neither side can be satisfied without violation of the other. Tragedy as a genre explores the conflict between private and public, expressed in terms of the sexual and the political.

For example, King Lear cannot politically succeed in dividing the kingdom as he sees he must do to guarantee peace in the future, and also possess Cordelia as if she were his consort. When he is forced to recognize the incongruity of the two aims, he blows up the whole scheme, turning to the worst political solution, dividing the kingdom between his two wicked daughters, and thereby guaranteeing future strife. When I say that Lear cannot both divide the kingdom and possess Cordelia, I want to emphasize Lear's well-thought-out plan to keep the peace. Dividing the kingdom as he planned, with Cordelia residing in the middle realm with Lear and his one hundred knights—and with her marriage alliance to Burgundy, the greatest force on the Continent—all makes excellent *political* sense; but it makes no sense psychologically, except as the expression of a wish. And it is a fantasy that Cordelia cannot participate in, for obvious reasons, not least her own sexual needs and aims as a young woman. When Lear's fantasy is denied by reality (both terms refer to sexual need), he assures future strife, exactly the opposite of his intention expressed when he appeared before all his courtiers with the map.

Oedipus cannot both rule in Thebes and possess the queen, at once the political leader, his wife, and his mother. In that sexual-political conflict there is to be found no resolution except death and banishment. The suffering of tragic characters, as Aristotle points out, follows from the conflict with inevitability, that is, no resolution is possible. There indeed is a source of pleasure for us, since we who sit in the audience recognize the inevitability and are granted godlike omniscience for a moment, the condition we all long for and are denied in political reality. A well-made plot that is structured in terms of sexual-political conflict moves to its conclusion with the certainty and inevitability of a logical syllogism. That inevitable march through plot—episode after episode—yields pleasure because we can *predict*, while the protagonist, whose quest begins the action, cannot foretell the outcome. The much-commented-upon tragic irony grants us a godlike power: we achieve immortal prescience, and that also grants us the "right" to *enjoy* the scene of pathos, that is, the scene of suffering at the end of the tragedy. Though woefully transitory, the power with which we are endowed by the drama stimulates a fantasy of omnipotence. And that gives us immense pleasure, though it is momentary. But when have we ever had the foresight to see beyond the pleasure of the moment?

Of course, we must concede at the end of the play that the tragic hero has perished, or has been vanquished by fate. The reflections we entertain outside the theater may therefore be woeful and depressed; there is a great gulf between the mania of witnessing and the depression of recollection.

As we see tragic action and choice unfold with inevitability, we experience that affective state Aristotle referred to as catharsis. Complex as it is, I think we can account for it in terms of the conflict I have singled out. We see and on some level (perhaps unconscious) accept the inevitability and irresolvability of the sexual-political conflict and its outcome in deep suffering. And the acceptance of the audience helps to define that much-argued-over term, catharsis.

We the witnesses, because of the prescience bestowed upon us, are free to accord the tragic hero an accommodation *in our awareness,* so that we provide a place to the deposed tragic sufferer who is the cast-out *pharmakos,* the polluted one. Tragedy enjoins us to entertain the stark realization that in the inevitability of suffering, justice drops away and becomes an unarguable issue. Tragedy rises above the whole question of justice—and I wonder if that is because the basic and generating conflict is truly unavoidable and the two sides irreconcilable. We therefore are led to become truly magnanimous observers, and *we* accord acceptance to the hero where justice in any ordinary, limited, political sense cannot be realized. We are enabled to grant a psychological acceptance to the inevitable conflict of the sexual and the political that we have witnessed. The ground for this, I believe, is that moral incongruities of an unacceptable kind—incest, parricide, violations within the family—reside within *us,* the audience, by the simple fact of our humanness. However Lilliputian our own strivings and our own terrors are in comparison with those of an Oedipus or a Lear or a Hamlet, we accord acceptance to these tragic heroes because of the revealed nature of the conflict, and we respond with a generous act that can only ennoble us to our own moral consciousness.

Tragedy draws moral distinctions that help us in growing up. In the character of Oedipus a distinction is drawn between those events, acts, and sufferings imposed by the gods and by fate, and the acts that are his own doing, flowing from self as a moral agent. After he blinds himself, Oedipus says: "It was Apollo, friends, Apollo, that brought this bitterness, my sorrows, to completion. But the hand that struck me was none but my own."

Irrational and rational forces in human conduct are also distinguished: there is the deep sexual force, uncontrolled, aroused, as if a madness sent by the gods; and there are the demands of political obligation, the demands for *deliberate,* careful choice as a conscious response to political reality. Oedipus comes to be seen as the tragic hero is always perceived: a mortal bound by fate, and a human being taking actions freely chosen with the aim of realizing the good. That the two aspects of human life interpenetrate and cannot be separately dealt with, or distinguished according to one's main concern, is one of the deepest recognitions of tragedy. It is a *recognition* as if it were a *recollection:* something we know in ourselves from the very earliest stages of cultural awareness.

My point is that psychosexual conflict, which sets private need against and in conflict with public political obligation, is at the very heart of tragedy: it is the source, the ground, the raison d'être for tragedy as a representational action in culture. The conclusion of the tragedy provides for us, generates in us, the pleasure peculiar to tragedy, as Aristotle puts it.[3] That is so not only because we see our predictions confirmed, but also because we are forced by the well-made play to accord an accommodation to the tragic sufferer. The audience as witness accords the protagonist a reconciliation, taking the character into the "community," now defined as the psychological space we inhabit as members of a political realm. We see the protagonist through beliefs about beneficence and nobility; and the hero's presence in the reality of the community—the reality of a dramatic festival, the reality of a *performance* in the city—accords the community the sacred aura of the mysterious sufferer, who is both blessed and cursed. In these terms we can understand that most mysterious of plays, the last play Sophocles wrote and the conclusion of the Oedipus story: *Oedipus at Colonus*, in which the city of Athens gains a kind of political immortality from the housing—the giving of sacred residence to—the body of the old, blind Oedipus, who then is raised up to the semi-divine status of *daimon*. This play is not a tragedy, but a paratragedy of the sort I have referred to in chapter 2.

Splitting

Underlying the presence in tragedy of riddles and the public-private conflict is the psychological process of "splitting," a term Freud introduced in his late papers. Our capacity as adults to enjoy tragedy, to find it pleasurable despite its horrors, rests upon splitting, a process that begins in play in the earliest stages of a child's life and continues to structure our relationship to objects throughout our lives.

In giving a brief account of splitting as a psychological force essential to our pleasure in the painful, I shall turn to the work of D. W. Winnicott, the English psychoanalyst, who introduced the idea of the transitional object. Dramatic enactments, such as tragedy, function for

3. "One must not seek any and every kind of pleasure from tragedy, but only the one proper to it" (Aristotle, *Poetics* 53b11).

us as transitional objects in the later stages of our development; the transitional objects Winnicott identified as a psychological and cultural necessity in the early stages of maturation continue to exercise their power, but in transformations that are unique to each cultural tradition. Tragedy in its Athenian mode is a unique discovery, but that does not imply that other cultures lack similarly functioning transitional objects.

In Winnicott's observations, "transitional object" refers to the objects children play with that help them to leave the mother, to move out to the world beyond, carrying, as it were, a bit of the maternal protection as safeguard. Of course, he was talking about blankets and teddy bears and suchlike; for us the important thing to note is what happens to these objects and the ways in which they enter into dramatic situations—how they participate in role taking and creation of character. Early transitional objects become participants in playacting, story telling, and a variety of exchanges between child and parent in the process of building a *cultural presence*. My extension and elaboration of Winnicott's views—moving forward to later stages of maturation and communal participation in the creating, sustaining, and interpreting of objects—introduces the idea of *cultural tradition* and the existence of a necessary ground for tradition, which can be thought of psychoanalytically as the narcissism of the group or community. To be *of a culture* and *in culture* requires identification with others and the others' identification with objects such that the self is known in part through and by means of the objects; the self gains some of its defining characteristics through the objects it possesses as its own.[4]

The name "transitional object" obscures an aspect of the developmental stages through which the object moves in its relationship to the playing child: the object becomes a subject. It takes on a character, even a personality, which endows it with personlike properties and opens it up to participation in fantasy life. Then the object as subject generates narratives. Mother and child tell stories in which the object-subject and

4. For Winnicott's views, see "Transitional Objects and Transitional Phenomena," *International Journal of Psycho-Analysis* 34 (1953): 433–56. Reprinted in *Playing and Reality* (New York: Tavistock Publications, 1982) 1–25. For my views on cultural objects, see *Psychoanalytic Theory of Art: A Philosophy of Art on Developmental Principles* (New York: Columbia University Press, 1983).

they themselves become characters. Plot, too, grows through a shared imaginative building of action. The object—toy, blanket, stuffed animal—now, as subject, transcends simple thinghood and becomes a character in a plot whose denouement mother and child devise. Winnicott develops the relationship between child and mother in the following way:

> From birth . . . the human being is concerned with the problem of the relationship between what is objectively perceived and what is subjectively conceived of, and in the solution to this problem there is no health for the human being who has not been started off well enough by the mother. . . . The transitional phenomena represent the early stages of the use of illusion, without which there is no meaning for the human being in the idea of a relationship with an object that is perceived by others as external to that being.[5]

It is through narrative *acted out*, as it is in dramatic representations, that the society carries forward the early experience of the child with story telling as a cultural event. It is through narrative, through representational capacities with which it is endowed by the mother and child, that the transitional object becomes a cultural object. Winnicott calls it "the first cultural object." Thus through closeness to mother and to thing metamorphosed into subject, the child is introduced to the rudiments of cultural life. I use the term "metamorphosis" intentionally, because that is the word recognized, with its attendant associations, from classical story telling as the process that symbolizes the entry of the person into culture. When an animal is changed into a person, a person into an animal, a frog into a prince, a charming story-teller into an ass—this is the traditional metaphor with which story introduces the child into a tradition of enactments. Indeed, that *is* culture: a tradition of enactments. And among enactments tragedy stands as monumental.

Risk is an aspect of transitional objects I want to draw your attention to: the danger in extending oneself to create character and plot, to es-

5. Winnicott, *Playing and Reality*, 11.

tablish *representations*. We see it happen readily, but it involves a certain courageous putting oneself outside of oneself, and therefore taking a risk. There is anxiety in taking a role, being a someone with another name, another origin, different parents; for it is establishing a different destiny for oneself. To change one's identify is to be set into a track leading to another end point in life. Tragic characters all take terrifying risks in their move towards an end point they believe they foresee, but that they come to see is false (as we the audience already know), false not because of ignorance, but because of limitations that are insurmountable *human* limitations. One unconscious purpose in devising plots is that we *believe* we transcend, in the very act of making a plot, the hiddenness of destiny. Thus the making of tragic art is itself a denial of the tragic content of the art work, in this case the performed tragedy. To attend the theater naturally follows play with transitional objects; to witness tragedy as a theatrical enactment expresses and grants communal authority to the wish to know our own fates.

In any case, the strong emotions Aristotle singled out—the feelings of *pity* and *fear*—are present and sometimes can be overwhelming when one engages in representations, as actor, as witness, or as responsible producer of the tragic drama. How do we cope with those strong feelings? For usually they do not overwhelm us as we watch; in fact, despite pity and fear, we experience "the pleasure appropriate to tragedy." How does that come about? How do we sustain ourselves in the course of the experience we have with such powerful objects and the emotions they generate?

In two late papers Freud speculated on the psychological process by which the risks and ambivalences of our experience with representational objects—transitional objects—come about. Employing the terms "split" and "splitting," Freud suggested in the uncompleted "An Outline of Psychoanalysis" and in the fragment "Splitting of the Ego in the Process of Defense" that we use splitting as a means to cope with certain basic situations of a threatening kind; I want to suggest that among those threatening situations are the cultural situations taken as the subject of representational objects in which human actions and human relationships—especially family relationships—are depicted.

Freud pointed out that splitting is a psychological process whereby we cope with threatening and anxiety-arousing situations. "Two psychical attitudes," he wrote, "have been found instead of a single one—one, which takes account of reality, and another which under the influence of the instincts detaches the ego from reality. The two exist alongside of each other." Splitting of the ego, Freud went on to say, characterizes many psychological processes; and we find, especially in psychosis and neurosis, that "two different attitudes, contrary to each other and independent of each other" are to be found in many interactions between the ego and external reality.[6]

Developing these views in one of his last papers, Freud observed that we see most clearly in children the capacity to tolerate "a conflict between the demands by the instinct and the prohibition by reality." (Note how this description parallels the conflict basic to tragedy, the conflict between sexual need and political obligation.) The child takes two positions at once and simultaneously and thereby, in Freud's terms, "splits the ego."[7] The child both turns away from reality and turns towards reality, thus resolving what appears to be a contradiction with simultaneous affirmations—an unconscious strategy, if we can call it that, of Lear in setting up the kingdom that not only was to survive him, but that he was to in a sense preside over from beyond the grave. In such early experience, and then in latter stages of development, we see the capacity to entertain both A and not-A, or the ability, in psychological terms, to entertain a fantasy alongside a realistic construal of the world.

Splitting represents a pathological defense; but as with so many such defenses, we find that there are developmental stages in the ways the primitive psychological process comes to be functional in culture. Splitting is a culturally essential psychic strategy that underlies our capacity to create and to respond to representations of all sorts, particularly works of art, or, as I call the wider class of cultural objects, *enactments*.[8] The healthy and maturationally coherent development of

6. Freud, "An Outline of Psychoanalysis," in *Std. Ed.*, 23:202–4.

7. Freud, "Splitting of the Ego in the Process of Defense," in *Std. Ed.*, 23:275–77.

8. There are cultural distinctions in the ways audiences participate in represented actions. To many cultures, the tragedies we honor and prize are barbaric, false, or simply nutty. See the delightful description by the anthropologist Laura Bohannan, "Shakespeare in the Bush," *Natural History Magazine*, 1966, Aug.–Sept. Cross-cultural encounters demonstrate the role of belief in the response to narratives.

childhood splitting is seen in our response to tragic drama—finding pleasure in that which also arouses deep anxiety. For in tragedy the audience is led to entertain two views at once, to split the ego, in Freud's words: on the one side the audience recognizes the dramatic reality—that *is* Oedipus, that *is* Hamlet; on the other side is the realization, always kept in delicate balance with the action, that the events are in some sense "play events," the characters "play characters." That mode of cultural perception marks the culmination of a developmental project. We see the stations of cultural maturation if we think back to childhood anxieties that the object-subject *is* hurt or lost or dead, and if we recollect the powerful emotions evoked by the simplest songs and stories through which as children we are inducted into culture.

Transitional objects, in the limited sense explored by Winnicott and in the broader sense suggested in this inquiry, become the first cultural objects, through splitting. The participants assume two positions simultaneously: they know the object for what it is; they also *deny* the everyday reality of the presentation because it is (and this must be learned) a *representation*. Story telling, whether in the simple mode of family play with objects or in the sophisticated mode of serious drama, relies upon the process of splitting for the special pleasure it engenders: the pleasure *appropriate* to tragedy. That pleasure is one to be *learned* through cultural induction, not a pleasure that is given at the start of life's journey.

One way in which pleasure is encouraged and allowed to be felt, is through the content and structure of the object itself, of the dramatic plot, for it employs the process of splitting. Riddles split meanings: for the question points in one direction, but is answered only by turning in a different—sometimes a shockingly opposite–direction. Psychosexual conflicts in the political domain of tragedy split actions and persons: the action undertaken to establish a political condition turns out to be an action to satisfy an inner need; and characters are represented with their doubles, surrogates, and foils, a fact evident from a name such as "Oedipus." In Aeschylus' *Seven Against Thebes*, the name "Eteokles" is matched with and against "Eteoklos," one fighter outside the walls, one fighter inside the walls of the besieged city. The furiously fighting sons of the split Oedipus are themselves split in name and in dramatic conflict. The play plays on splitting; the audience responds with splitting and reconciliation of the divided objects.[9]

Splitting occurs in the riddle through revealing and concealing: the manifest revelation is an answer that seems to solve the riddle; the manifest answer is split off from the latent, contrary implication that the riddle *betrays* but does not *parade*. "Betray" has two meanings here: the first is to show or indicate what is not obvious; the second is treachery, fraud, violation of trust. And that is what the riddle of the Sphinx forces us to recognize—a betrayal, in the sense of delivering over to the enemy, the enemy being the deepest truth about ourselves as human. Thus poor Oedipus, the solver of the riddle, is *betrayed*, for the answer that is hidden (we would say *repressed*) is just this: "Oedipus." In his response to the riddle, Oedipus splits his name, as we have noted; he fails to make the connection between "swollen" and "knowing," a connection *in the name itself*. The two meanings are separated by a phoneme, but that is the deep way of human language: in its slightest modulations it conveys the deepest truths. Here is a treacherous slip, a fatal slip, more grievous than the slips Freud examines in *The Psychopathology of Everyday Life*. Oedipus splits his sexual self and his ruler-political self, as indeed we all do to some extent.

The splittings I have pointed out are not kept apart by the plot of the tragedy, but are allowed to merge, to reveal or *betray* themselves, or, finally, to *parade* themselves. That occurs in the scene of suffering, which Aristotle recognizes as essential to the highest form of tragedy. Here that mysterious pleasure of catharsis occurs. At that moment, we the audience are allowed a perspicuous awareness in which both sides of the split are manifest: here before us is one person with one fate. Thus the meaning of *fate* is put in a new light: it is the confluence, the bringing together of two chains of causal action initiated with one end in view. For Oedipus, one end is political power, success in rule, sexual potency; the other—not in conflict with the first, as far as he can see— is to be the good ruler, the one who will save the city, the one who will identify the source of pollution. In pursuing the two different goals, he is pursuing one goal. The split existed from the beginning in Oedipus'

9. Helen Bacon discusses the many presences of splitting in *Seven Against Thebes*; see her notes to the translation by Anthony Hecht and Helen Bacon (New York and London: Oxford University Press, 1973).

view of himself and his mistaken beliefs about his past; the split is healed in the scene of suffering with the attendant catharsis at the end of the play. The answer to the riddle now becomes two in one, one in two: it is humankind and it is Oedipus. The knowing one and the swollen-foot are one and the same.

We are left with the problem: What *is* the pleasure appropriate to tragedy? It is not the pleasure of religious lustration, of medical purgation, of pressing grapes or olives—all contexts in which catharsis is used as a literal and a metaphoric term. Since tragic drama elicits powerful emotions that are painful in other contexts, to experience the pleasure appropriate to tragedy suggests that the feelings are manipulated in a way peculiar to this kind of representation. For there are many representational effects that are revolting and thoroughly unacceptable—we see them every day on television and in the movies.

I think the deepest psychological process that creates the pleasure appropriate to tragedy is splitting. And it is the means to the mastery of splitting that yields the pleasure we find in the harshest scenes of suffering. It is the mastery of this process and the knowledge it makes manifest that allow us to become cultural beings. To be sure, we discover and, as it were, grow into the pleasure appropriate to tragedy at a late stage in the process of becoming cultural beings; it succeeds much simpler and simplifying views of ourselves we hold in earlier stages of maturation. The process of growing into culture begins with transitional objects; it ends with tragedy. That could be a parable of the human condition: from teddy bears to Oedipus.

The deepest truth in tragedy is in the represented cultural conflict between the sexual and the political. This conflict drives the action forward; this is the initiating condition; this is the forever mysterious and secret inner life of tragedy because it is the secret inner life of human beings. The conflict drives the action to its "end," which always implies a death because it is the drive in human life that can end only in death. This is not to reassert the drive Freud referred to as the *Todestrieb*, or "death-drive," but to give a reason—if one can be given—for the *necessity* that offers us, the audience, our moment of prescience, as it fills us with the sense of how physical, how bodily, how *carnal* we are as human beings . . . the sense that under the plots and the temperaments and the defense of virtues, there is the sheer bodily beginning and ending of a life. That, as we saw, was the latent tragic insight of *The Merchant of Venice*.

Of course, tragedy as a cultural expression is dangerous. To find pleasure in depictions of suffering may make us all bad citizens in two respects: we may become hardened and indifferent and cruel; and we may turn away from political life in despair and opt out for contemplation, gurus, and repression. Psychologically, we may deny that there are political obligations at all, and feel that only the sexual matters. That may be one of our problems today; in fact, both dangerous consequences are represented in our lives as citizens in modernity. That opens up an avenue of inquiry appropriate to modernity: can the tragic understanding of the great dramatists be enlarged and extended in modern philosophy and in the story telling of our own time? This chapter leaves us with that question as the next puzzle, the next riddle to be examined in the next few chapters, following the riddles of pleasure in the painful I have been trying to solve.

4   Quest for the Sublime:
Philosopher as Tragic Hero

A Stupendous Vision of Diameters

                      Emily Dickinson

It is time that beats in the breast, and it is time
That batters against the mind, silent and proud,
The mind that knows it is destroyed by time.

                      Wallace Stevens

Modernity has endowed the artist with qualities of tragic heroism, in the process altering forever the basic design and deepest insights of traditional tragedy. With modernity from the Enlightenment to our own time, the political-sexual conflict has been repressed and the field of conflict resurveyed, reboundaried, given a new order of play.

We today continue to celebrate "genius" as if it were protagonist in a cultural drama to which we all are the audience. But our conception of genius has a somewhat different focus from that of the Enlightenment and its Renaissance inheritance: we emphasize the "art-life," a cultural object itself synthesized out of biography and works, drawn together into a grand design that creates a tale with a rich content of actions and objects in their presumed interrelationships.

Aware of the emergence of the art-life as a cultural reality, philosophers of art were quick to conceive themselves as competing heroes exemplifying the process of growing up in culture. The artist *made* objects, the work of genius, the objects *of* culture; the philosopher, through moral and aesthetic sensibility, lived through stages of self-consciousness expressed in acts of interpretation. For art needed philosophy, since philosophy somehow "explained" art. Philosophy, the philosophers seemed to be saying, makes plots and characters, just as dramatists and novelists do.

The philosopher as hero was established by Plato when he memorialized Socrates in the dialogues; since that most remarkable conjunction of the poetic and the philosophic—especially in the *Phaedo* and the *Phaedrus*—no dramatic representation of the philosopher has in any degree approached the classical genre. Modernity, as is its way, worked a variation on the ancient topos: the developmental stages of reflective philosopher-characters as they matured towards full self-consciousness became the stuff of the intellectual *Bildungsroman*. In this form the philosopher returns as hero, and the modern philosopher takes *himself* as subject matter. Modernity defines itself through self-representation both in art and in philosophy.

It is in the European Enlightenment that the philosopher as hero makes his comeback. Some revel in self-advertisement, like Rousseau; others discreetly don the mantle of scientific modesty, but their narcissism peeps through—as with Kant. It is one of Kant's distinctions to have reorganized the whole of philosophical interpretations of the beautiful by placing, at last, the appropriate emphasis on objects, the products both of nature and of art.

Aesthetic theory in early modernity had little difficulty accommodating art and nature to a distinction that today we find hard to draw. One kind of experience, one kind of object, one kind of form was referred to by the terms "beauty" and "the beautiful," while another kind of experience, object, and—by contrast—mysterious formlessness was referred to by the terms "sublimity" and "the sublime." Although we today regard the distinction as dated, it reflects, I believe, an ever-present conflict both within and without experience when we human sensibilities confront objects. The conflict and the internal states of awareness became one of the dominant themes in nineteenth- and twentieth-century art. I shall create a diorama for our exhibition of philosophical heroism in which the central character is Kant's representation of philosopher as hero.

I

Kant's *Critique of Judgment* states the distinction between beauty and sublimity in its most powerful form, with philosophical awareness of the implications for objects as they work for us in modernity. Although Kant's interest in the distinction was stimulated by his analysis of Newtonian science and by the demands of his moral theory, the metaphysical interpretation given to beauty and the sublime enabled him to "save" religious longings in the face of the destruction of traditional "proofs" for God—one of the inevitable consequences of modernity—and the denial of beliefs about individual survival after death. We may not feel those problems acutely, but the Kantian analysis bestows upon us, in this later day, a number of benefits.

If we recognize, as I do, that the philosophical interpretation of art underwent a revolution in the transformation that occurred between the thought of Kant and the thought of Hegel, then we can see the first benefit conferred by the beauty-sublimity distinction: it was the avenue of escape from symbol theories of art that dominated the making, use, and interpretation of art from the time of the church fathers into the eighteenth century. For the first time since the Augustinian theory laid down rules of how to interpret icons and texts, the experience of art was thrown into the domain of feelings. Now a variety of subjectivisms were tried out, and the way was cleared for expression theories of the sort we see in our own day, through modernity into the postmodern era. One way for our time to look upon the *Critique of Judgment* is this: it genuinely demythologized painting, poetry, and architecture. That opened the way to the establishment of a general theory of culture and an account of the expressive powers of cultural objects. The life of feeling counted as much as the ingenuity of interpretation; the sentimental wove its colors and sounded its tones throughout the adventures of the hero—especially the philosopher as hero. The context shifted from church and Bible to culture and art, from tragic hero caught in a web of fate to modern intelligence solving problems. On the surface, Kant's grand philosophy is a splendid optimism. Covertly, it challenges the myths that provided the foundation for tragic plots. Demythologizing implies, among other things, a change in the content of art, what art is about. For one thing, art can now be unashamedly about art. (Of course, art is always about art, but there is a difference between what one can profess—or might confess—and that which authority approves.) For another, art can drop old themes and assume new ones; there can then emerge a self-conscious formalism and aestheticism, one of the characteristics of modernity.

The second benefit conferred by the beauty-sublimity distinction is this: by throwing the experience of art into subjectivity, we can discuss and respond to art in terms of pleasure and pain. The way is open to all the *expressive* dimensions, such as the expression of the artist, the expression of the work, and the expression of the beholder in responding to the object. The audience expresses itself in witnessing, as the artist expresses self in creating. And the audience can declare itself—as John Dewey had the American brashness to do—an artist in its own right.

The third benefit derived from the distinction between beauty and sublimity is that a certain kind of experience is sought and prized, the experience we refer to as "romantic" and associate with an artistic movement, romanticism. Heightened sensitivity, extremes of expressive affect, and feelings communicated in an explosive act—all this is summed up in Baudelaire's description of Delacroix's achievement. Delacroix has interpreted better than anyone else, maintains Baudelaire, "the invisible, the impalpable, the dream, the nerves, the *soul*."[1]

Fourth, the beauty-sublimity distinction allowed religious values to be seriously considered, but in an altered form that did not violate assumptions about the impossibility of using traditional religious arguments. The fact that experiences of sublimity were related to mystical experiences allowed the philosopher to hold on to an important dimension of experience without having to make certain assumptions about

1. In Baudelaire's letter to the editor of the *Opinion Nationale*, 1863. Printed in "The Life and Work of Eugene Delacroix," in *The Mirror of Art*, ed. and trans. Jonathan Mayne (New York: Anchor Books, 1956), 309. Goethe said of Delacroix's illustrations for *Faust*: "Delacroix is an exceptionally gifted artist who has found in Faust a theme after his own heart. The French frown on his impetuosity but here it is exactly what is wanted. . . . This artist's soaring imagination compels us to think out the situation as thoroughly as he has thought them out himself. And since I'm bound to admit that in these scenes mon. Delacroix has surpassed his own vision, it's even more certain that, thanks to him, my readers will find them more vivid, more compelling than anything they'd picture to themselves." Quoted in Pierre Courthion, *Romanticism* (Cleveland: 1961), 60–61.

the supernatural. At the same time, the emphasis on a natural mysticism, if I may call it that, led to other difficulties not encountered in a supernaturalism—for example, the need to confront the failure of religion. This failure is the loss Melville bewails in *The Confidence Man*, discussed in chapter 6.

The problem of beauty—understanding its symbolic and expressive import—is now cast into a modern form. Traditionally, beauty could be related to God's design and handiwork; in the development of modernity, beauty becomes a subjective response and is differentiated from the sublime. The beautiful and the sublime are now—in the Enlightenment—treated as different kinds of experience, often in conflict with one another. Yet this modern way of conceptualizing experience confers benefits upon the philosopher, who now can take up, in his reappearance as hero, a new and exciting dialectic. The human search for beauty, driven by a deep, unconscious need, comes unexpectedly upon the sublime, and the encounter is like meeting the serpent in Eden. It calls upon the philosopher to do battle with forces outside of ordinary experience. The capacity of art expands to take in this new confrontation and the intense affects it generates. As the philosopher's artistic fantasy will show us, modernity creates cultural objects with an intensity that at first was frightening, so frightening it called forth aesthetic restraints. Thus the beauty-sublimity distinction serves modernity, which on the one hand has grown to prize the aesthetic above all other experiences, and on the other has gone in search of extreme emotional experiences through which the philosopher could explore the boundaries of human existence.

Finally, a fifth benefit conferred by the distinction between beauty and sublimity is the capacity to account for and to use the *unconscious* in the making of cultural objects and to recognize the unconscious as a necessary aspect of the interpretation of cultural objects. There is, then, a psychological understanding that is articulated in the distinction. This insight first expresses itself in the identification of the sublime as a cause and as an effect (for the term is used to refer to both sides of the relationship between object and person). The sublime *causes* fear, awe, dread, heightened awareness; the sublime is also an effect, an experience to be set alongside and contrasted with the beautiful. We today see the workings of the sublime—both as cause and as effect—as a symbol of the unconscious forces we draw upon in the making of art and respond to in the interpretation of art. The philosopher, then, has a heavy task in offering a theory of the sublime; Kant does not explore the complexities of the experience with sufficient depth, though he provides a "map" that we may use to orient ourselves, as we, in our postmodern skepticism, somewhat disdainfully read Goethe's *Sorrows of Young Werther* and celebrate Wordsworth's *Prelude*.

In *The Birth of Tragedy*, Nietzsche reasserted the distinction through the categories of the Apollonian and the Dionysian. Today we rely upon a different set of categories for our way of thinking about beauty and the sublime in their psychological dimensions: the categories of conscious and unconscious, of ego and id, of expression and repression, and of secondary- and primary-process thinking. These terms, the products of psychoanalytic theory, refer to forces, processes, and aspects of experience that have been used in modernity and postmodernity to establish the distinction between the beautiful and the sublime.

II

At this point I think it necessary to describe and give a brief analysis of the beauty-sublimity distinction as it was formulated in Kant's influential *Critique of Judgment*.[2] In my presentation I shall go beyond anything Kant explicitly said about the relationship of beauty and the sublime. I begin with fundamental beliefs about art and nature.

Both nature and art, when composed in perspicuous forms, induce the special, complex experience we refer to as "the beautiful." The philosopher's primary concern is to separate the internal feelings we have in the presence of the beautiful from the internal feelings that obtain for the theoretical, the moral, and the merely subjective feeling of pleasure. The argument can be simply stated: the predicate "is beautiful" is appropriately applied to an object when the experience of the object meets specific conditions laid down in the "Four Moments of Taste." By "four moments of taste" Kant refers to the four basic aspects of a uni-

2. Immanuel Kant's *Critique of Judgment* was first published in 1790; a second edition followed in 1793. It was translated into French as early as 1796, with subsequent translations in 1823 and 1846.

fied experience of a natural or created object. The four moments are: that we feel subjective, yet disinterested pleasure; that we are disinterested in the object as utilitarian or simply as an existing thing; that we attribute purpose to the object, though without being able to state conceptually what that purpose is ("purposiveness without purpose" is Kant's striking phrase); and that we assume others can make the judgments we make in the same situation, though they may not, as a matter of fact, do so. In short, Kant imaginatively projects a *community of aesthetic sensibility and capacity to respond,* rather like the one he has already projected for the ideal of moral freedom. Judgments of beauty follow from delight in nature and from our capacity to respond to nature represented in art, just as judgments of moral qualities follow from a common endowment of will and reason.

In contrast to our experience with beauty, the human responsiveness to sublime experiences and the need to search out the sublime in both nature and culture follow from our natural longing for the unconditioned, for that which transcends experience. Even in the study of nature through the sciences, we express a longing for answers to questions that lie outside of experience: questions having to do with God, freedom, immortality, and the ultimate conditions of cosmic creation and annihilation. But a close study of the limits of human knowledge leads us to see that we can never possess answers to such questions. In short, metaphysical questions have no meaningful answers—or, worse, every answer is "true."

Yet the urgency to find answers to ultimate questions persists; the search continues and expresses itself in a variety of ways—for example, in religion, in the pursuit of metaphysics, and in the experiential encounter with nature. Answers are required by a side of human nature, the ethical side, that cannot be suppressed: in moral striving, in everyday moral judgments, we regard ourselves as members of a moral community in which we are free to choose, to act, to will the good, and to act in conformity with universalizable laws. We not only seek the unconditioned in experience (we are, this philosophical imagination insists, by nature romantics), but we require some assurance of its possibility in our moral lives, else we are reduced to beings situated in a universe of causal necessity, denied our freedom as moral beings. The universe according to Newton is not a universe in which *human* beings can feel at home.

Our desperate search for the unconditioned is doomed to failure, and in this fact lies Kant's tragic view of life. The basic conflict is generated by a science that alienates us from nature and a moral imperative that separates us from our affective selves. Underlying Kant's analyses of experience is a deep pessimism, however much his expressed doctrines insist upon a discovery that will save religious beliefs and values, for no Pietist could consciously accept the tragic as part of the human condition. One way for us to place Kant's philosophical enterprise in the study of tragic heroism is as a series of evasive and consoling arguments—many of them derived from the arts themselves—that will allow us to feel *at home* in nature and with ourselves. At-homeness is the ultimate condition that the *Critique of Judgment* strives to establish through strenuous argument.

Thus tragedy is consciously avoided, and the dominant spokesman for Enlightenment modernity creates an exhibit that allows all of us to overcome the anxiety of tragedy through a reinterpretation of beauty and the sublime. Grasping the evidential straw of beauty, the philosophy floats off into one of the loveliest fantasies of all human speculative history. That fantasy postulates beauty as a symbol of morality and buries the tragic beneath a monument of argument. The encounter with beauty reassures, soothes, creates an at-homeness that we treasure; yet in the search, especially as we tramp through nature's landscapes, we come upon the sublime. That moment blasts the order and harmony of beauty, only to strengthen the philosopher's resolve to make the destruction of beauty through the force of the sublime once again evidence that the human situation can be one of comfort. For the sublime experience is direct evidence of a supersensible, unconditioned realm, a reality that will put to rights all the fatefulness of ancient tragic conflict and reaffirm religious beliefs lost in a Newtonian devastation.

The philosopher performs poetic heroics at this moment of interpretation, working a metamorphosis upon experience that establishes philosophy's power to encroach upon the domain of poetry. Kant's vision executes a feat very like the one performed a few years

later by Wordsworth in *The Prelude*. Indeed, Kant seems to have anticipated Wordsworth's autobiography:

> Fair seed-time had my soul, and I grew up
> Fostered alike by beauty and by fear . . .
>
> (*The Prelude*, 1, lines 301–2)

The interpenetration and balance of beauty and the sublime described
by Wordsworth are exactly what Kant seeks to understand in the *Critique of Judgment*.

I shall make conscious the repressed Kantian fantasy of philosopher
as hero in my own reconstructive way, different from the way Kant
would prepare an exhibit of his images; the way I tell the story of the
beautiful-sublime is close to the narrative explored in *The Sorrows of
Young Werther* and *The Prelude*.

As a novelist, Kant might have written the story thus: The journey
of our lives begins in the theoretical (empirical) realm of nature, where
we judge in terms of space, time, and the categories of the understanding, such as number and causation. Even in the early stages of our
maturation we feel the tug of spiritual longings, faint yet persistent.
Forces moving us towards the unconditioned intensify as we grow up to
encounter the complexities of moral awareness and attempt to integrate ourselves into a moral community in which we necessarily
assume that in some hard-to-define sense, we must postulate our freedom from the theoretical (empirical) domain. Thus, as adults, we
confront a deep split in our cultural life, with science on the one hand
and morality and religion on the other. Philosophers, having analyzed
the traditional theological arguments for the existence of God and the
destiny of humanity, must reject such supposed arguments; yet all of
us find ourselves with the need, growing more and more urgent, to find
some basis for a congruence between Newtonian science and our moral
consciousness.

It is in the experience of beautiful art and beautiful nature that we
first dimly realize the possibility of a congruity between our theoretical
selves and our moral selves, or to put it institutionally, between science
and morality-religion. The intense subjective pleasure we take in the
beautiful is sharpened by its implications; indeed, it occurs to us that

beauty is a symbol of morality. The excitement and exhiliration following upon the mysterious symbolization (one is reminded of the mystic's ecstasy) fill us with energy that we, today, can refer to as "romantic," in the historical and poetic sense the term has accumulated. At last we see a way to defend the belief (heretofore seemingly irrational) that there is a compatibility between our theoretical and our moral natures. Our longings for the unconditioned, though no firmer in their scientific ground, still gain a credibility through a condition we come to enjoy: we feel at home. We *feel* the universe made for us, we for it; we reside in it as our home.

I have called this Kant's "novel" not only because it is the heroic tale of the philosopher as hero, but because it is a worthy—indeed, a necessary—exhibit in the progress of tragedy in modernity. Kant's novel is a cultural object, and it expresses the condition of all cultural objects: they exist both within and without space and time. The novel is really an account of the hero's encounter with space and time, and it can be read as the lifelong experiment conducted by everyman: the human effort to be freed from entanglement with the spatiotemporal order. Since the genre of the novel as a cultural object and product of the Enlightenment is an art most intimately involved with space and time— and established the means to represent them—its substance is its form and its form is its substance. The novel, therefore, is the most apt representation of the argument Kant formulates in the *Critique of Judgment.* Between the novel as cultural expression and the experience of the encounter with beauty and sublimity, there is a deeply gratifying congruence.

I now undertake to retell Kant's philosophical "novel" as a tale of space and time; told this way, the deep beauty-sublimity interconnection, in its philosophical interpretation and in its novelistic representation, emerges with an aesthetic clarity.

The hero of Kant's tale is the philosopher-knight doing battle with space and time. The first encounter takes place in nature structured as a mechanical system of strictly determined causal events. Not only must the Knight accept the Newtonian mechanistic description of nature, but the encounter itself impresses upon the hero his finitude and impotence in the natural order. Space and time coerce the Knight, almost aborting the quest, but he perseveres with the stern determination we see in Dürer's engraved hero, rather than with the fateful blindness of the tragic hero of the distant past.

The second exploit carries our hero outside space and time altogether, for the moral life, the next stage of maturation, can be conducted only on the assumption that some part of the self enjoys an uncoerced existence. Freely the Knight performs his moral exercises and wins renown. But at this stage he more and more resembles characters in fairy tales, overcoming obstacles in an imaginary-magical way, and slipping, very like Don Quixote, into storybook reality. The adventures in the realm of freedom allow the Knight to break the barrier of coercive causality in mechanistic nature, to return to a nature transformed into the aesthetically beautiful, which gives subjective pleasure. Now nature brings joy, and the anxiety of hopelessness is subdued; experience in both the theoretical and the moral realm begins to give way to feelings of at-homeness. For though the moral realm may welcome the Knight as a member of a Kingdom of Ends, it is yet not his true home, for it is shared with other rational beings whose moral excellence far exceeds that of the Knight. He longs, as we do, for the human as human, the realm made for *us*.

To be once again at home, the hero must return to nature, to spacetime, and to the pleasures that are peculiarly, uniquely human. The Knight recognizes return when his response to nature is to nature not as a causal determinism, but as a beautiful scene in which he takes delight. Now the prowess of the Knight is revealed, for he takes the experience of beauty in nature and through the gift of *genius* turns it into art. Our Knight, as so often in stories of adventure, is really the artist. Now at last he dwells in nature made conformable to his needs, and his art coerces nature, forcing it to give him pleasure. No longer is he dominated by the laws of nature, no longer is he internally compelled by the moral claims of reason; now his genius *gives the rules* to nature, and the Knight is free to respond to the beauty of his realm. Art has made nature conformable to our deepest needs as human beings, for it satisfies the need to be at home in nature, and at the same time it gives intimations of congruity between our theoretical and our moral selves. The split between science and religion, between determination and freedom, between alienation from nature and at-homeness in nature, has been overcome. Happy reconciliation!

However, there is, as always, a worm in the apple of felicity, for the experience of beauty carries with it the dangerous possibility—indeed, as we come to see, the inevitability—of nature's other side revealing itself. Nature—wild, untamed, and, in our Knight's words, both "mathematically and dynamically" sublime—poses the last obstacle to a happy ending for the Knight's tale. For a moment the minor strain of the tragic is heard! For nature confronts the Knight, both in extent and in force, as beyond the capacity of human sense and understanding to comprehend and structure it.

In the words of our hero: "We may describe the sublime thus: it is an object of nature the representation of which determines the mind to think the unattainability of nature regarded as a presentation of ideas." Thus nature remains for us, however heroic our efforts, a reality above and beyond sense and understanding, connected somehow to a super-sensible, or *noumenal*, realm. Though nature, in its sublime presentation to us, boggles, yet it intimates: the sublime is an intimation of a reality beyond sense. That the Knight cannot capture the sublime through his genius in art now becomes clear, but there are artistic sub-limities that imply the ultimate reality as a reality that can be entertained: Wordsworth's *Prelude* and Goethe's *Faust* explore the ex-periential structures that bring beauty and sublimity into a dynamic triumph over denial and meaninglessness. And the Knight, in his ad-ventures, shows us how this is achieved.

The final chapter in Kant's novel might be called "The Knight's En-counter with the Sublime and How He Copes with This Fearful Confrontation." Kant writes the episode this way (though I shall read it another way): When the Knight encounters the sublime in nature, he is forced to pull back; to defend himself, he asserts his moral superi-ority to the powerful, huge, uncompassable sublime, to that which Emily Dickinson refers to as "A Stupendous Vision of Diameters." The Knight's defense against the threat of annihilation, against the anxiety generated by an indifferent universe, is to retreat, psychologically speaking, to his moral nature, that which lifts him outside space and time. Thus he "saves" himself with the thought that, however nature in its raw indifference deals with him, yet he is superior to its un-developed consciousness.

My telling of the critical episode in the Knight's adventures is differ-ent: if the Knight performs as Kant relates, then our hero is not fulfilling his genius as an artist; for art does not retreat to moral supe-riority, but takes the encounter with the sublime in one of two ways. Either art reaffirms beauty and through the beautiful reforms terrify-ing nature, or art, in the hands of the highest genius, represents the sublime through symbolic intimations. Modernity invented aesthet-icism and romanticism as means to these ends.

Kant's novel has come to its end, and though it flags with the Knight's moral defense, it gives a philosophical rendering of the con-flict between beauty and the sublime, as well as some insight into the stages of human maturation that allow the Knight to cope as well as he does. The "Critique of Aesthetic Judgment" (part 1 of *The Critique of Judgment*) thus takes its place as a *Bildungsroman* (a novel of growing up) with the philosopher as knight-hero. The philosophical novel of growing up provides more than a knight-hero; it gives us a series of stages of cultural development to complete the theory of transitional objects as written by Winnicott. In that perspective, Kant becomes therapist to modernity's anxiety of alienation. His "cure": simple aes-theticism through beauty, beauty as a transitional object that moves us outside of the coercive, destructive, uncompassable "diameters" of space and time, into space and time as restructured for our delight. In short, we are returned to the Garden of Eden before the Fall. Thus trag-edy is repressed; but only for a moment, for the beauty of nature is periodically overwhelmed by the sublime—the ever-present annihila-tion of the self. *Et in Arcadia ego:* even in the mythic eternity of the Garden of Eden, death hides; for however we force space and time to give us delight—as surely we humans do in our capacity to respond to and create beautiful objects—we are devoured by time. The philoso-pher felt the desperation induced by "time that beats in the breast;" philosophical argument succeeded in transforming time from Newto-nian absolute time to Kantian time-for-me-in-the-beautiful—yet even intellect wholly pure and sincere could not overcome time, for the mind knows it is destroyed by time.

What a contorted retelling of the tragic tales this is. But perhaps all modernity skirts and scants the tragic whenever possible and substitutes for it a compromise formation, because of a repression. Yet, as we know, modernity has reconstructed the tragic in a variety of substitute formations, some of them shockingly violent.

III

Surveying our exhibitions of the tragic hero in modernity, we revel in the sublime, barbaric images for which Delacroix's art can stand as the best representative. His pictorial adventures were aptly characterized by Baudelaire: "The morality of his work is also visibly marked with Molochism. His works contain nothing but devastation, massacres, conflagrations; everything bears witness against the incorrigible barbarity in man."[3] Delacroix would have been the ideal painter to depict the repressed Kantian hero, as he in fact did represent the adventures of the hero Faust. But the violence of the sublime was much modified, toned down, not only by the genteel philosopher, but also by the novelists who, in the early years of modernity, carried the beauty-sublimity conflict to new domains that required subtlety of representation because the tragic was not considered a proper subject for bourgeois entertainment. Not long after Kant defined the sublime experience as an integral, yet subversive, force in the human effort to make nature conform to *our* wants and needs, the novelist Jane Austen, in *Sense and Sensibility*, brilliantly and subtly dealt with the oppositions of art and nature in the setting of the drawing room. She translated cosmology into psychology.

Building slowly through complex encounters between characters, an outburst of narrative rage suffuses the conventional proprieties of *Sense and Sensibility*. Rage is the sublime force that disrupts the beautiful surface, rage the cosmic energy behind the appearance of the world. In the novel, our entertainment is a walk through a beautiful landscape—until we come upon a dispossessing violence that drives us away, denies us the beauty of form. Both within the drawing room and out in the garden, at-homeness can be frighteningly disrupted. Rage, like fate, dispossesses, bereaves us of our home place.

3. Baudelaire, quoted in Mayne, "Delacroix," 327.

The novel is full of dispossessions. The Dashwoods are forced to leave their house as the story opens, and finding a place in which to be at home is a search that goes on in external space and in internal time. Both in nature and in manners, the young Dashwood women are woefully vulnerable. Three passages in *Sense and Sensibility*, in chapters 17 and 18 of volume 1,[4] introduce the basic conflict as it is played out first in nature, then in society, and finally in the moral life, where a betrayal has destroyed a possibility for love. The tragic may be repressed, but anger brings it back into consciousness.

In the first passage, Edward remarks to Elinor as they walk out of doors: "I like a fine prospect, but not on picturesque principles. I do not like crooked, twisted, blasted trees. I admire them much more if they are tall, straight, and flourishing. I do not like ruined, tattered cottages. I am not fond of nettles, or thistles, or heath blossoms. I have more pleasure in a snug farmhouse than a watch-tower—and a troop of tidy, happy villagers please me better than the finest banditti in the world."

In the second passage, Elinor and Marianne exchange views on money and happiness:

> "What have wealth and grandeur to do with happiness?" [asks Marianne].
> "Grandeur has but little," said Elinor, "but wealth has much to do with it."
> "Elinor, for shame!" said Marianne; "money can only give happiness where there is nothing else to give it. Beyond a competence, it can afford no real satisfaction, as far as mere self is concerned."
> "Perhaps," said Elinor, smiling, "we may come to the same point. *Your* competence and *my* wealth are very much alike, I dare say; and without them, as the world goes now, we shall both agree that every kind of external comfort must be wanting."

Nature, money, and, as the next episode to be quoted will show, love are the three levels of reality that the novel explores, on each level revealing the destructive force that lies underneath a surface order. Actors in the drama live in fear as they seek comfort, for appearances

4. Jane Austen, *Sense and Sensibility* (New York: New American Library, 1961).

are masks, and the experiences of the Dashwood family members are, in every case, instances of unmasking.

In the sequence of scenes, the episode first quoted, in which nature is the object of analysis, is followed by this one, in which a deep betrayal bobs to the surface of a conversation that begins in a superficial politeness and control. We should keep before us the reference to nature in its controlled beauty and uncontrolled wildness.

> The subject was continued no further; and Marianne remained thoughtfully silent, till a new object engaged her attention. She was sitting by Edward, and in taking his tea from Mrs. Dashwood, his hand passed so directly before her as to make a ring, with a plait of hair in the centre, very conspicuous on one of his fingers.
>
> "I never saw you wear a ring before, Edward," she cried. "Is that Fanny's hair? I remember her promising to give you some. But I should have thought her hair had been darker."

Edward answers that it is his sister's hair, and the passage continues:

> Elinor had met his eye, and looked conscious likewise. That the hair was her own, she instantaneously felt as well satisfied as Marianne; the only difference in their conclusions was that what Marianne considered as a free gift from her sister, Elinor was conscious must have been procured by some theft or contrivance unknown to herself.

Sense and Sensibility explores the beautiful surface and the violently sublime hidden depths of nature, of money, and of love—natural, social, and psychological necessities through which we establish ourselves at home in the face of forces that make the achievement of such composure hazardous. Although Jane Austen is not ordinarily regarded as an artist with a developed tragic sensibility, I find that her representations contain the beauty-sublimity distinction and are fully aware of the conflicts that generate tragedy. There is a latent content in *Sense and Sensibility*, expressed through the symbols in the three quoted passages, that allows us, the readers, to bring into consciousness a fundamental relationship—that between nature, money, and love.

The social surface masks a hidden reality that *Sense and Sensibility* brings into consciousness.

Some twenty years after *Sense and Sensibility* was written, a short set of youthful reflections on nature, money, and love was being written out privately by Karl Marx, later to be published as the *Economic and Philosophic Manuscripts of 1844*. The philosopher's reflections make manifest much that is latent in the novelist's plot. It is significant that Marx's observations draw heavily upon literature, quoting *Faust*, *Timon of Athens*, and other texts that relate money to love. The young Marx was as aware as Austen of the ways in which modernity had rewritten the themes of tragedy.

Marx begins his observations with a repetition of the idealistic point, clearly articulated by Hegel, that human feelings and passions "have by no means merely one mode of affirmation, but rather . . . the distinctive character of their existence, of their life, is constituted by the distinctive mode of their affirmation."[5] Modes of affirmation vary within modernity, as they do from one cultural epoch to another. Marx and Austen formulate the beauty-sublimity antagonism in different terms, by means of different symbolic representations, and with varying degrees of hiddenness and secrecy. While Marx is explicit, Austen is subtle; yet they both are determined to represent a deep underlying reality of human social life.

Marx writes with a novelistic flair: "Money is the *pimp* between man's need and the object, between his life and the means of life. But *that which* mediates *my* life for me, also *mediates* the existence of other people *for me*" (137, Marx's italics). Because of this power, money can turn every kind of condition—social, sexual, proprietary—into its opposite.

> If I have no money for travel, I have no *need*—that is, no real and self-realizing need—to travel. . . . Being the external, common *medium* and *faculty* for turning an *image* into *reality* and *reality* into a mere *image* . . . *money* transforms the *real essential powers of man and nature* into what are merely abstract conceits and there-

5. Karl Marx, "The Power of Money in Bourgeois Society," in *Economic and Philosophic Manuscripts of 1844* (Moscow: 1959), 136. Page numbers hereafter cited in text.

fore *imperfections*—into tormenting chimeras—just as
it transforms *real imperfections and chimeras*—essential powers which are really impotent, which exist only
in the imagination of the individual—into *real powers*
and *faculties* (140, Marx's italics).

Now Marx approaches directly the issues represented and interpreted
in *Sense and Sensibility*. Even the discussion of the beautiful and the
picturesque participates in Marx's depiction of the power of money;
only money can so transform—or fail to transform, if it is lacking—
the landscape. For what is the exercise of human control over nature,
where the object is the beautiful—private delectation and pleasure—
but the exercise of wealth?

Marx concludes the analysis with a sentiment quite common, even
banal, and to that degree true: "Assume *man* to be *man* and his relationship to the world to be a human one: then you can exchange love
only for love, trust for trust." If we could inhabit a world without money, we might be true to one another as human being to human being;
yet that is a condition to be realized only in a state of primal generosity,
if such can be imagined. It is the innocence and sincerity Marianne
longs for and Elinor realizes is a fantasy, an expression of a wish. Elin-
or's sense of the condition of human life shaped by money, as described
by Marx, becomes a harsh, perceived reality when the plait of hair in
Edward's ring presents itself as the symbol of duplicity and falsehood
in their youthful relationship. Just as nature is transformed through
landscape gardening, so human nature is deformed through the pursuit
of wealth. Love becomes subordinate to money. The contradiction now
becomes plain to all the youthful characters in the novel: sexual longing and companionate marriage cannot be realized where society is
shaped by money. Both Marianne and Elinor must relinquish their
true feelings—sentimental and moral—to the exigencies of the power
of money. Into the imagined social felicity of the Dashwoods comes as
a destroying force the sublime recklessness of social position, wealth,
and imposture; in response to that intervention, all relationships
among the characters are changed from what is wished to what is required. Thus the conflict between beauty and sublimity finds a special
Austenian form: sensibility, moral conscientiousness, love, and trust

are sacrificed to a certain "Molochism," to the "pimp" between human need and objects in whose presence the cultural tradition has been perverted. Society's once-open recognition of tragic circumstance and tragic suffering is forced into a latent tension, like a concealed volcano; and over it all a smooth grassy turf is cultivated.[6]

The reality of subjugation to objects at last induces the appropriate response in the rage expressed by Marianne and Elinor in volume 2, chapters 12 and 13. Only Elinor is allowed to vent full narrative consciousness, because she has had to confront the duplicity of the Ferrars.

Edward has secretly allied himself with Lucy, provoking this thought in Elinor, a thought that comes directly from the text without the mediation of conversation: "Elinor's curiosity to see Mrs. Ferrars was satisfied. She had found in her everything that could tend to make a further connection between the families undesirable. She had seen enough of her pride, her meanness, and her determined prejudice against herself, to comprehend all the difficulties that must have perplexed the engagement and retarded the marriage of Edward and herself, had he been otherwise free." In the social world of *Sense and Sensibility*, pursuit of the beauty of romantic ideals and sincere moral actions out of high principle is frustrated by the economic, or bourgeois, sublime, if I may call it that. Accommodation to this terrifying experience takes the form *not* of a retreat to moral isolation in one's moral superiority, as with Kant, but rather the form of submission and subordination of women to men.

Sense and Sensibility constructs for my collection a modern tragedy in the Kantian mode. Tragic coloration suffuses the narrative canvas through the creation of a plot representing stages of growing up, a plot every bit as profound as Kant's, with a truer denouement. One way to classify the representation that is *Sense and Sensibility* is this: it is the telling of the tale of the beautiful and the sublime under a Marxist revisionism.

Allowing the young Marx to enter Austen's drawing room introduces the philosopher as bully where he has been explicitly uninvited; yet from Kant's account of how the beautiful and the sublime interact,

6. The image of the volcano comes from Emily Dickinson, some of whose thoughts will be considered in the Epilogue. Dickinson wrote a series of volcano poems, about which I have written in *Psychoanalytic Theory of Art*.

we can learn to read the tragic plots of modernity, as Marx perceived them. Adding his direct vulgarity to Kant's romanticism, we can see that there *is* tragedy where we thought there was something we have referred to as "comedy of manners." Such a misapprehension expresses a reader's repression as response to a novelistic repression, for contradiction and repression work together as modern psychological forces to obscure loss and the pain of mourning.

5   Modernity Interprets Tragic Justice: Reading *Michael Kohlhaas*

Fiat iustitia, pereant iusti

Modernity, in the Kantian imagination, was energized by a Newtonian vision of the universe, which imposed upon us a belief in a hidden reality beyond human sensory capacity. Modern psychology, imitating the epistemology of Newtonianism, energized by a Freudian vision of psychic life, sought the secret inner of experience, analogous to that outer postulated by a science of nature. Thus bracketed between beliefs in two unknowables, suspended in a phenomenal world of limited sense awareness and limited inner awareness, we today find ourselves sentenced to the hard labor of discovering by various inferential methods the realities without and within.

In this study I have been pursuing tragedy, one kind of poetic fiction that emphasizes our suspended place between the realities of hidden outer and hidden inner. We today, in rearousing tragic mysteriousness, make far more of tragedy than it ever consciously tried to make of itself. And in our modern reconsideration of the classical topoi, the strangeness of justice has received special emphasis.

Justice, an object of reflection from ancient through modern narrative forms, has often been regarded in its presence and in its power as mysterious. It was Kant among the moderns who forcefully articulated the nature of justice and its transcendent source: a presence in the human realm that brings with it an otherness, an intimation of its source without our world; a mysterious intervention, as if a numinous presence of a noumenal reality. Only a few philosophical studies explore the strangeness of justice; far more is it appreciated by storytellers such as Heinrich von Kleist. He obsessively pursues the strangeness of justice in the story *Michael Kohlhaas,* the next exhibit in modernity's way with tragedy.

We postmoderns have lost our orientation; the political realities of the past frequently drop out of consciousness. But we must appreciate Kleist's attention to the harsh realities of Kohlhaas's political world. If we are to integrate the action of this nineteenth-century story into our reflections on tragedy, we must confront Kohlhaas's happy acceptance of a conclusion that to our fictional sensibilities can only appear paradoxical. We must make the connection between the character Kohlhaas and the Reformation. And we must make the connection between Kleist's world and the story set in the past—his past—that he chose to tell. Finally, we must position ourselves towards both narrative realities as they look back to tragedy.

If all that is accomplished, the story functions for us as a transitional object. In a manifest sense, it transports us from one reality to another. But in a deeper, latent sense, the story is a transitional object as Winnicott used the term, for it allows us to venture forth from the legalistic world of writs and trials, punishments and rewards, to experience with some sense of conviction the realm of the unconditioned that Kant postulated to be the highest manifestation of reason. Our journey towards that goal will be as full of strangeness as is Kohlhaas's very own story.

I

The opening sentence of *Michael Kohlhaas,* shocking in its concision and conclusion, ends with the two terms that most precisely characterize a tragic hero: "einer der rechtschaffensten zugleich und entsetzlichsten Menschen seiner Zeit."[1] As one of the most "upright" and "terrible" men of his time, Kohlhaas is introduced in both his classical mythic and historical modern aspects. (The term *entsetzlich* conveys a degree of inner feeling on the part of the speaker that the English term "terrible" lacks; perhaps the term closest to the German is the one used by Sophocles to describe humankind: *deinon,* which

1. Heinrich von Kleist, *Michael Kohlhaas* (Stuttgart: Reclam, 1971). Passages in English are from Martin Greenberg's excellent translation in *The Marquise of O and Other Stories* (New York: Ungar, 1973). Page numbers from both editions hereafter cited in text.

conveys a sense of skill, wonder, and the uncanny, as well as the horrifying.) The protagonist of tragic drama is both just and terrifying; the protagonist of this story, we are told, was before his thirtieth year a model of a good citizen ("das Muster eines guten Staatsbürgers" [3]). After his exemplary young manhood, he was to become part of the peasant insurgency that helped to bring justice into the modern state; yet within this narrative of events, justice remains problematic and deeply mysterious. In several respects the hero's search for justice seems to coincide with the search of the traditional tragic hero; yet in other respects, Kohlhaas seems to be fundamentally different.

Kohlhaas, we are told, "carried one virtue to excess"; the implication is that virtue, in Kohlhaas, is extravagant and eccentric, and that therefore his actions will be seen under the light of a peculiar goodness, for virtue is a good of character. But in this case the good of character draws round itself an aura of uncertainty, for it contributes to the characterization *entsetzlich*. Kleist gives the hero the following description: "Die Welt würde sein Andenken haben segnen müssen, wenn er in einer Tugend nicht ausgeschweift hätte. Das Rechtsgefühl aber machte ihn zum Räuber und Mörder" (3). ("The world, in short, would have had every reason to bless his memory, if he had not carried one virtue to excess. But his sense of justice turned him into a brigand and a murderer" [87].)

An *excess* of virtue—justice, goodness of character, or any other virtue—would ordinarily be regarded as a contradiction: how could one be *excessively* just? Presenting this virtue as a limitation or defect in Kohlhaas suggests that he was concerned *only* with justice, and therefore neglected or failed to realize other virtues he ought to have cultivated as a good *Staatsbürger*. As I reflect on the character of Kohlhaas it occurs to me that he calls upon me to think of other characters of whom it might be said that they are "excessively" just. I think about other characters entangled in the labyrinth of justice: Antigone suffered from an excess of justice; Shylock destroyed his family, his religious privacy, and himself through obsessional dedication to justice; perhaps God is excessively just. Are they so filled with the unslaked thirst for justice that they will destroy to realize it? Are they immune to the countervailing passion of mercy? However, the provocations to justice in the older exemplars are different from those in our case, for our hero had such a fine sense of justice that it drove him to become a robber and a murderer. And that sense was not roused in him, nor did he take vengeful actions, until justice was denied *him*—until he was, by his own interpretation of events, cast out of the state.

This appears to be a distinguishing condition separating our story from traditional plots and characters. Since justice was denied him, Kohlhaas took justice into his own hands, and in so doing he became an unjust man. How can that be? If justice was denied *him*, does it not follow that he had no obligation to be just to others? Yet in the end justice was done and Kohlhaas accepted it joyfully. How strange.

The depths of strangeness to which *Michael Kohlhaas* conducts us has affinities with the strangeness we know in Sophocles' *Antigone*. Both plots force us to recognize the ambivalence of human being and human action: we live by law and custom; we violate law and custom. Joining ourselves within community and then separating ourselves from community expresses the strangeness that in extreme cases arouses dread. Reflection upon this feeling preoccupies several of our profound plots; it generates philosophical reflection.

The chorus in the *Antigone* sings: "There is much that is strange, but nothing / That surpasses man in strangeness." To this, the German philosopher Martin Heidegger responds:

> The strange, the uncanny [das Unheimliche] . . . is that which casts us out of the "homely," i.e. the customary, familiar, secure. The unhomely [Unheimische] prevents us from making ourselves at home and therein it is overpowering. But man is the strangest of all, not only because he passes his life amid the strange understood in this sense but because he departs from his customary, familiar limits, because he is the violent one, who, tending toward the strange in the sense of the overpowering, surpasses the limit of the familiar [das Heimische].[2]

These are frightening words when uttered by a German philosopher who wholeheartedly gave himself to the Nazi party and its realization

---

2. Martin Heidegger, *An Introduction to Metaphysics*, trans. Ralph Mannheim (New Haven: Yale University Press, 1959), 150–51.

of the most dire human depravity. In his mouth, they celebrated the violence of Nazi Germany as it surpassed "the limits of the familiar." But our story is far removed from that; it is in spirit and understanding close to *Antigone*. Our romantic hero suffers tragic strangeness and acts out the tragic violence in a story that assumes a modernist perspective on a story from the past, and represents once again a character from the past in modern guise. *Michael Kohlhaas* undertakes a deep renovation on an inherited plot.

The political reality in which Kohlhaas's character has been shaped is this: justice was bestowed by the state; justice was withheld by the state. And that reality took shape before our hero's very eyes. Kohlhaas set out to market to sell his horses, met opposition to free passage along the road at a tollgate, had two of his horses forcibly kept at the castle controlling the tollgate, and was told that he could retrieve the horses when he had received from the governmental office in Dresden the proper "pass."

Kohlhaas returned with the pass, only to find that his groom had been attacked—almost killed—and the horses (his two "blacks") virtually ruined by field use. From that point onward Kohlhaas had one goal: the restoration of his blacks as fat, unblemished, and "glossy-coated" as they were the day he set forth to market. Justice is restoration.

Our modern plot exhibits a trajectory wonderfully different from the classical; yet covertly, slyly, Kleist has insinuated the classical into the modern, exposing the reader to a strangeness of aesthetic form that mirrors the strangeness of philosophic thought. In *Kohlhaas* the movement is from law-abiding citizen to outcast and then back to law-abiding citizen. The outcome of the plot is that the horses are restored and Kohlhaas, to answer the demands of justice, is executed. Think this plot upon the model outlined by Aristotle in the *Poetics*. There is a curious modern deformation that yet preserves the basic tragic elements. The hero of a tragic drama always begins as "law-abiding" in some sense, falls away, and then returns; but the "return" is effected through the audience granting the hero *its* acceptance. In *Kohlhaas* the "acceptance" is bestowed by the state itself. I shall point out such differences as we go along.

Since tragic plots possess an initiating event lying outside the boundaries of the plot, there must be an initiating event for *Michael Kohlhaas*. The initiating event in this modern "tragedy" is the holding of horses as security until the horse dealer returns with the pass. In this case, it seems to me, we must look to history, for the demand to pay a toll and to present a pass threatens the free market the horse dealer enjoyed before the story opens. Furthermore, turning the horses to field work, using them *for* work, converts them from objects suitable for exchange into economic instruments. It is in the deterministic embrace of history that our plot finds its necessity, for neither fate nor Kohlhaas's character is responsible for the ultimate outcome. The wily conspiracies of the nobles—pure human perversity—weave a web of duplicity around Kohlhaas's efforts to find justice, while his character, in contrast, is hesitant and judicious. Some striking characteristics of Kohlhaas as hero are his even-tempered nature, his tranquillity when first challenged, and the impulse to see good wherever he looks. Even provocation at the castle does not draw forth anger from him, but a willingness to see the seeming slight put to rights. He has a childlike trust that justice will be done.

After going to the horse fair in Dresden, Kohlhaas learns that the demand for a pass was a fable (*Märchen*). On his return to Tronka castle (the site of the tollgate where he left the horses), he experiences only the bitterness one feels at the ordinary sufferings one is subject to ("als das der allgemeinen Not der Welt"). Even when he sees his worn-out horses, he is not sure an injustice has been done. His sense of justice is so fine that he requires a great deal of evidence before he concludes that he has been wronged: "Doch sein Rechtsgefühl, das einer Goldwaage glich, wankte noch; er war, vor der Schranke seiner eigenen Brust, noch nicht gewiss, ob eine Schuld seinen Gegner drücke . . ." (9). ("But his sense of justice, which was as delicate as a gold balance, still wavered; he could not be sure, before the bar of his own conscience, whether the man was really guilty of a crime" [93].) Kohlhaas's dedication to truth is as strong as his sense of justice. He appears before us always stating the reality. When the Junker comes into the yard of the castle, Kohlhaas says: "Das *sind* nicht meine Pferde . . . Das sind die *Pferde* nicht . . . Ich will meine wohlgenährten und gesunden Pferde wieder haben" (10). ("Those are not my horses . . . those are not the horses . . . I want my well fed and healthy horses back!" [94].)

Compare this declaration and the claim that follows it (I *will have* my horses back just as they were) with the search on which a protagonist in classical tragedy sets out. The quest is undertaken to rectify a wrong, to reestablish justice where justice has been denied or contaminated. Sometimes a particular object must be recovered, and in the quest for the object the true nature of the disturbance in the polity is revealed. Discovery depends upon the hero's knowledge coupled with a private preparedness to accept reality; but often, especially at the initiating choice, reality is denied. Discovery of the true state of affairs may hinge on wit: a riddle is posed and its answer sought. Indeed, as I suggested in chapter 3, the riddle appears to be a constant in all tragic plots; the riddle will make a strange appearance in Kleist's plot, too.

Kohlhaas fragments the traditional structure and redistributes the elements dislodged from their usual sites. The resolution of this plot requires the restoration of objects to the condition they were in previously. Physical things play an essential part in this "tragedy," for they stand as metaphors of moral regeneration. The outcome that resolves the conflict (the two blacks are restored to their original condition) coincides with giving the answer to the riddle, which, oddly, is possessed only by the protagonist and never revealed to the reader. Reading *Kohlhaas* is like looking at a traditional tragic plot through a kaleidoscope.

The riddle, posed as a reply to a burning wish on the part of the Elector to know the fate of his noble line, is given to the Elector by the Gypsy, a character appearing late in the story: "From what direction does the danger to my house come?" The answer is written down by the Gypsy: "All right. I will write down three things for you: the name of the last ruler your house shall have, the year in which he shall lose his throne, and the name of the man who shall seize it for himself by force of arms" (171–72).

The knowledge sought by the Elector—the knowledge possessed by the Gypsy and passed to Kohlhaas on a scrap of paper, which he reads and swallows—is the possession of the future every mortal wants to control. With this knowledge, Kohlhaas has at last subdued time, has made time conform to his wish: he has restored the past (his horses are

restored just as they were), and he knows the future. Gaining both justice and foreknowledge grants Kohlhaas the two conditions mortals
most want and despair ever to achieve. The two are deeply interrelated;
if we have foreknowledge, then we can solve the riddle of justice.
Human beings who knew the future would know either that the future
is rigidly determined (in which case justice is the shadow of an empty
wish) or that they are free to control events through choice, in which
case justice would stand as a realizable idea of reason, in Kant's sense—
that is, an ideal to be postulated, though not finally proven. Foreknowledge indeed might allow any one of us to die content.

But the confusing tumult of the closing scene delivers us to a bit of
recognition of our own, as if a private message: as we witness the exchange of a life for foreknowledge and the restoration of physical
objects, we hear a murmur from the Gypsy. If we achieve the constancy
of the past, coerce the universe into a unique retrogression, then a terrible price must be paid for the violation; we are amazed to see that
Kohlhaas is indeed willing to die for that minute constancy. That seemingly small demand—that the two blacks be restored to their former
condition—is the tragic protagonist's call for a reversal of all that tragedy has established in its painful history: that human efforts to deny
fate constitute violations of cosmic and communal justice.

It has often been pointed out that violation of natural or divine order
is a prerequisite for the event that initiates tragic plots. In traditional
tragedy the violation usually occurs before the action of the drama; but
in *Michael Kohlhaas* the violation occurs at the conclusion of the story,
and like the tragic hero of old, Kohlhaas pays the price. Curiously, what
Kohlhaas sought was not possession of the future, but rather the restoration and constancy of the past. He was granted both, for he achieved
restoration of the physical objects taken from him, and at the same
time he was given foreknowledge. Thus we can say he "triumphs" in a
way no hero ever has: he restores the past and comes into possession of
the future, and for that he gives his life. What is it that we hear in the
strange final scene?

To realize justice, to set the communal order to rights, stands as the
duty of an Oedipus, a Hamlet, or one of many other tragic protagonists; Kohlhaas's service to justice seems no less. But Kleist's hero
is a protagonist living out his destiny in a modern state; this is not the

aristocratic ruler whose duty is defined by elevated rank and inherited authority. Kohlhaas is the *Staatsbürger*, the common merchant, the law-abiding citizen. Yet his quest is for a justice as absolute and universal as any dreamt by a philosopher. His sense of justice is conveyed to us by the metaphor of the delicate sensitivity of a gold-weighing instrument. We can project that image of scales to society as a whole. And then we see Kohlhaas suddenly taken out of the grand panoply of the closing scene, a scene like a crescendo of grand opera, and squeezed back into the consciousness of Kleist, who treats Kohlhaas as if he had internalized a set of principles that we from our present vantage point see as the consequence of the Enlightenment. Kleist takes a story derived from and set in the Reformation and endows Kohlhaas with foreknowledge of the revolution to come. Indeed, Kohlhaas's foreknowledge participates in that document of the revolution, the Declaration of the Rights of Man and of the Citizen. Its insistence that human beings possess the right of property, the right of equality, and the right of security rings throughout Kohlhaas's rampage of revenge. In this respect, our hero's search for justice carries him into the future in a very real historical sense that does not ordinarily qualify the quest of the tragic hero. Yet this way of interpreting the story relates its conclusion to an ideology that really does not work affectively in our experience of the story. What, then, in terms of feeling, is the crucial difference between justice as the goal of classical tragedy and justice as the realized end of *Michael Kohlhaas?*

One obvious answer has to do with the way pathos is realized at the conclusion of the two sorts of plots. The scene of suffering, so moving as the conclusion of tragic action, hardly seems to figure in our story. The modern hero, the hero of modernity, who seeks justice in the modern state, acts under the rule of moral duty: we are obliged, Kantian moral theory advises, to adhere to the moral law regardless of happiness. Yet Kleist's hero finds that adherence to the moral law brings him happiness as it brings him death.

We are confronted with two kinds of pathos, that of the traditional tragic hero who is driven to violence, and that of the modern *Staatsbürger* who yields everything for the law—to the point of dying for justice. Yet Kohlhaas surmounts the second kind of suffering, for he dies willingly, happily. There is no scene of suffering at the end of the story, and although we may discover in ourselves an impulse to sadness, the evident joy of the hero puts us into a curious kind of stasis. We suffer affects that are quite unlike those that conclude our experience of tragedy. We are not allowed to feel any of the emotions we might expect to feel because of the events of the story. Thus we are not allowed to feel sorrow at the death of Kohlhaas's wife, since she has been granted another incarnation, or so it is implied. Nor are we allowed to entertain the Christian mortification that she, Lisbeth, counsels Kohlhaas to impose on himself: forgive and do good to your enemies, to those that hurt you.

Although the affects attending scenes of suffering are denied us, we begin to experience early in the story, and with increasing intensity as the story develops, a feeling about justice that is a part of the tragic representations against which we measure the modern *Michael Kohlhaas*. This feeling shapes itself around objects rather than points of view. For there are a variety of views on justice exhibited by the different characters. Kohlhaas seeks a state that will protect his rights and extend protection to all. Lisbeth believes one ought to turn the other cheek, accept the commandment to do good, and forgive those who hurt you. The Junker represents the haughty indifference of the stronger who defines right in the exercise of power. Finally, Luther, theologian and representative of divine vision, sees state law as subsumed under divine law such that if there are inconsistencies, the moral commandments of Christian obedience take precedence over the right to political complaint. To Luther, the supernatural realm reinforces the state, so that if the Archangel Michael (as Kohlhaas refers to himself) were to bring fire and sword against the state, God's anger would oppose the destruction.

Although the central issue in *Michael Kohlhaas* is the nature of justice, the representations and explorations of that problem are realized through a fanatical attention to objects rather than to ideas. All of Kohlhaas's energies focus on the two horses; they are magical and mysterious; they assume larger and larger proportions in our feelings as the story goes on, until they fill the world with their hugeness, as if they are presences from another realm. It is the feelings generated by their mysterious importance that both distinguish our story from traditional tragedy and, at the same time, endow our story with a complex set of feelings that play off against one another to produce a powerful sense of the uncanny. Yet the increasingly intense affect is not without its comic aspect, wonderfully presented in the last reference to the horses. They are restored physically and spiritually, since "a banner had been waved over the horses' heads to make them honorable again" (181). Comical as this may seem, it condenses a series of individual actions encountered throughout the story from which something weird peeps out at us. And the closing scene flashes with the presence of uncanny powers that all along have been crackling about the narrative hulk, encircling it as if with a strange St. Elmo's fire.

II

The conclusion of *Michael Kohlhaas* might be described by a parody of the phrase *fiat iustitia, pereat mundus* (let justice be done, though the world perish) as *fiat iustitia, pereant iusti* (let justice be done, though the just perish). As soon as we entertain the epigram, the strangeness that differentiates our story from classical tragedy becomes clear: classical tragedy culminates in a restitution that follows with necessity and seeming inevitability from the initiating event; it can accept the destruction of the world. By contrast, *Michael Kohlhaas* fails to establish necessity and the feeling of inevitability; it forces us to face a paradox: justice requires that *the just* perish. Thus the feelings we are subjected to at the end of the story—its catharsis, as it were— are of a different kind from those we suffer at the conclusion of traditional tragedy.

Two feelings dominate us at the conclusion of the story: an intensified feeling of the uncanny and of the mysterious forces that heighten the sense of the uncanny throughout the story; and a feeling I can only describe as a distancing, a feeling of alienation from the conclusion that strikes us as so irrational at the same time that it is received by the hero with joy. Both strands are woven into the *strangeness* of the story: strangeness in the sense of feeling *estranged* and strangeness in having to accept irrationality. Yet we *believe* the conclusion in the sense that we accept it as belonging to the world of *Michael Kohlhaas*. Our capacity to believe the conclusion as the realization of justice is prepared by the carefully controlled affects, which support and reinforce one another. The feeling of alienation—yet accompanied by belief—and the feeling of the uncanny are related in a deep way that can be understood, I believe, through some of Freud's comments on these feeling states.

Freud's speculations on alienation (*Entfremdungsgefühl*, "aliena-tion of feeling" or "derealization") and his analysis of the uncanny (*das Unheimliche*) are found in two separate papers. In the first, a letter to Romain Rolland in 1937, Freud recounts an experience he had when visiting Athens. Standing on the Acropolis, he thought, "By the evi-dence of my senses I am now standing on the Acropolis, but I cannot believe it."[3] Such palpable contradictions in experience cannot be ex-plained simply in terms of the present; Freud speculates that there must be a reaction to something in the past that contradicts or throws into doubt the present experience. The unconscious conflict leads us to articulate and hold in consciousness an absurd contradiction. There is a range of such experiences in which doubt attaches to different objects. Freud gives a brief description: "These phenomena [*Entfremdungsge-fühl*] are to be observed in two forms: the subject feels either that a piece of reality or that a piece of his own self is strange to him. In the latter case we speak of 'depersonalizations'; derealizations and deper-sonalizations are intimately connected."[4] Both experiences result from the effort to "keep something out of us," and they are to be contrasted with experiences such as déjà vu, in which we "seek to accept some-thing as belonging to our ego." Both inclusions and expulsions of these sorts are common ways we have of "keeping something away from the ego"; they are defenses. I shall argue, bringing together Freud's re-marks on *Entfremdungsgefühl* and his essay on *das Unheimliche*, that in both cases the defenses are common reactions to fictional represen-tations.

The feelings Freud experienced when standing on the Acropolis ("it is real, yet I don't believe") take the obverse form when we read *Michael Kohlhaas*. We think, "The events in the story are unreal, yet we believe." We, too, sustain a contradiction in our experience. We know the story is a fiction, yet it persuades us in a mysterious way, so that we believe the description as a plausible account at the same time that we would deny its reality. The nature of this response to narrative

3. Freud, "A Disturbance of Memory on the Acropolis," in *Std. Ed.*, 22:243.
4. Ibid., 245.

fiction—the *defining* response to narrative fiction—gives grounds to add to Freud's list of alienating and integrating experiences the sorts of encounters and responses we have with narrative fiction. These are *narrative realizations of fiction,* and they take the form of belief and unbelief in forceful opposition. (There is, I think, a contrary experience in the reading of history, which I would call *narrative derealization of history.* Modern novels and the cinema often present the past in a "derealized" form.)

How, then, does *Kohlhaas* achieve its establishment of belief? I think Freud is of help here. The thesis he proposes in his essay "The Uncanny" is that feelings of the uncanny are induced by events that match or confirm a thought, wish, or fantasy that has been repressed. The encountered event then leads to the "belief" that what was feared or desired is confirmed, and we think, "It is really true that such and such occurs." For example, we think, "It is really true that the dead come back to life; that mysterious forces pervade the universe," and the like. In our story, a similar confirmation is entertained: we believe it really is true that we humans possess a noumenal (suprasensible) existence that, just as Kant said, intervenes in everyday causal determinism.[5] Fiction generates such beliefs, and Freud saw the similarity between fiction and "real" life:

> The uncanny as it is depicted in *literature,* in stories and in imaginative productions, merits in truth a separate discussion. Above all, it is a much more fertile province than the uncanny in real life, for it contains the whole of the latter and something more besides, something that cannot be found in real life. The contrast between what has been repressed and what has been surmounted [Freud means here those beliefs that have been tested in real life and about which we have some

5. It may seem odd to suggest, as I intend to here, that the sober Kant paved the way for the uncanny as a popular theme in nineteenth-century German literature. No philosopher has a more developed sense of the experience of the uncanny than does Kant, whose whole analysis of experience insists upon the hidden, noumenal source for much that we believe, though it lies outside the competence of the understanding to prove. Just the conditions under which the predicate "is beautiful" can be properly applied introduce the conscious-unconscious split needed for the uncanny to enter into our awareness (see chapter 4).

> empirical confirmation.] cannot be transposed onto the
> uncanny in fiction without profound modification; for
> the realm of phantasy depends for its effect on the fact
> that its content is not submitted to reality-testing. The
> somewhat paradoxical result is that *in the first place a*
> *great deal that is not uncanny in fiction would be so if it*
> *happened in real life; and in the second place that there*
> *are many more means of creating uncanny effects in*
> *fiction than there are in real life.*[6]

Michael Kohlhaas demonstrates that indeed there are many more
means of creating uncanny effects in fiction than there are in real life,
for the story confirms deeply held, and for many readers unconscious,
beliefs about both the external world of physical reality and the internal
world of psychic reality. The fictional means and the psychologically
deeply affecting ends are clearly revealed in this story. By compelling
us to assent to deeply held beliefs in their reanimated form of fictional
narration, they work as means of inferential transport, carrying us out
of the suspended middle realm we inhabit in everyday life and into the
outer, ordinarily concealed, realms from which we draw imaginative
sustenance.[7] The experience of the uncanny works in ways not analyzed by Freud's inquiry, for the experience we have in successfully
realized narrative fiction connects our wishes and fantasies to the further realms of physical and psychological reality, which Freud (like
Newton) assumes we reach merely by means of the interpretative
methods established in the sciences. But that is the assumption of the
scientific inquirer attempting to confirm hypotheses about physical
and psychic reality. Freud points out that in our everyday lives we
make the inferential moves in deeply *unscientific* ways, through affective means, establishing connections often on the basis of inner needs.

Longings for transport to realms beyond experience—seemingly realized in experiences of the uncanny—are satisfied through fictional

6. Freud, "The Uncanny," in *Std. Ed.*, 17:249.

7. In this respect, Kleist is Kantian in a way he probably did not suspect. He was a
close reader and student of Kant, and much in his writing turns out to be, as in
Kohlhaas, a subtle posing and examination of problems for Kant's theories. Here is
another case for the claim that modernity sees the reanimation of philosophy and
poetry as competitors in the analysis of cultural reality.

accounts that function for us as transitional objects. It is an odd consequence of the Newtonian revolution, and Kant's poetic response to it, that modernity has elevated fictional narration to an eminence as great as any it has ever enjoyed. Rather than diminish or obliterate or derogate story, modernity prizes them all the more because of the death of metaphysics. Modernity respects and depends upon fictional narrations; I characterize them as transitional objects because there has been a profound change in the way the linguistic arts function today, as compared with periods of the past.

Winnicott argued that transitional objects function for young children as the first cultural objects; I extend the term's application beyond anything he discussed. Just how succeeding cultural objects, such as narrative fiction, also perform as transitional objects Winnicott did not attempt to work out; but his observations on children's play are suggestive, and they now can be further expanded when placed alongside Freud's speculations on the uncanny. For Freud's analysis of uncanny objects and the experience they induce defines a class of cultural objects whose *transitional powers* are exceptional. And *Michael Kohlhaas* is rich in that class of objects.

For a fictional narration to function as a transitional object, it must represent the process of transition through objects, as it itself serves to realize that function for the hearer or reader. Our story achieves that, I believe, by casting intense light upon physical objects. For example, Kohlhaas's insistence that his horses be restored and his conviction that the past can be reconstituted confirm beliefs we hold about the world, even though, if pressed, we would deny them. Kohlhaas expresses a complex interweaving of infantile and mature beliefs to which we respond on the level of our own unconscious beliefs.[8]

There is a childish denial of reality by Kohlhaas—a quality of character that gives him great force—and because of that, when he demands and insists that his horses be restored "just as they were," we are thrown into an anxiety of contradictory feelings: can we demand of

---

8. It is perhaps worth noting a linguistic parallel between our story and the dramatic tragedy *Othello*. In both, the term "ocular" occurs: Othello demands of Iago "ocular proof" of Desdemona's unfaithfulness (3.3); and Kohlhaas must make an "ocular inspection" ("Okular-Inspektion") of the horses to remove all doubt as to their identity (140–41).

justice that objects be restored *just as they were?* If the world allows this, then we can feel a joyous expectancy that we once had as children, but gave up as we grew up. We know that what Kohlhaas demands cannot come about; yet we *believe* it can come about, and we enjoy the pleasure of that belief. The story imposes its truthfulness upon us, but a truthfulness that fills us with a joyous dread. The total presentation generates an acceptance in the face of the impossible. The story becomes a myth, a myth of the moral life, as much a mythic representation of morality as Kant's *Metaphysic of Morals,* in which the idea of pure duty generates in the reader a feeling of the uncanny. Fiction reinforces and confirms the dreams of philosophers.

Indeed, fiction confirms history. Kohlhaas's exploits are part of the unrest we refer to, with the usual concealing generalization, as the Peasant Wars. We are told at the beginning that this is the historical setting of our story; once this period is established for the pillaging and burning we witness, the story is tugged away from the grip of myth and drawn towards the public realm of events confirmable through other sources. As a metaphoric bridge, as a transitional object in the expanded sense I am proposing, the narrative convinces us of its truth because it can move not only from narration to repressed belief and wish, but also from fiction to a coherence with outer, historical events.

Kleist convinces us that the source of violence is both external and internal by sounding one of those sentences only he can orchestrate; we hear it as if it were the tone of an instrument spun out above the orchestra. "Sobald der Hügel geworfen, das Kreuz darauf gepflanzt, und die Gäste, die die Leiche bestattet hatten, entlassen waren, warf er sich noch einmal vor ihrem, nun verödeten Bette nieder, und übernahm sodann das Geschäft der Rache" (29). ("As soon as the grave mound was raised, a cross planted on it, and the funeral guests gone, he flung himself down once more before his wife's now empty bed, then set about the business of his revenge" [111].) In one sentence Kleist focuses all Kohlhaas's inner compulsions. Justice may be his aim, but private loss gives power to his acts, the first of which is to attack Tronka castle in the hope that the Junker Wenzel von Tronka can be killed. Kohlhaas succeeds only in killing the brother, but the horses are found and saved from the fire that burns the castle to the ground. There follows a detailed description of Kohlhaas's wreaking destruction and death upon the villages, caused by "the hell of his unslaked thirst for revenge" (115) ("die Hölle unbefriedigter Rache" [35]).

His thirst for revenge intensifies; whole communities are razed; an army of vengeful, dispossessed peasants follows Kohlhaas, now become a political force terrorizing the countryside. He assumes the name and stature of the avenging angel, referring to himself as "a viceroy of the Archangel Michael, come to punish with fire and sword for the wickedness into which the whole world has sunk, all those who should take the side of the Junker in this quarrel" (121).

Kohlhaas's fury threatens to destroy the communal order of rule by rank and estate, yet political upheaval gives him no satisfaction for the wrong he has suffered and in no way moves towards restitution of the past. Only a supernatural force can requite the wrong, and thus we might believe, as does Kohlhaas, that the spiritual estate could intervene. Seeking a higher tribunal, stung by a manifesto issued by Martin Luther, Kohlhaas is driven to his most daring exploit: he disguises himself to gain access to the theologian and confronts him in his study. The bereft rebel believes Luther may command a power higher than that commanded by the Elector.

The fictional Martin Luther is a real character in the historical sense of "real." We know him from documents and from reconstructions historians make. Meeting Martin Luther in the story, we think, "So there really was a Martin Luther." It seems strange to put it that way, as if fiction could confirm and verify history, yet fiction does just that. Dubious reality is given substance through indubitable fiction. That apparent contradiction—that we should believe what is not "true"— renders Luther's presence in the story uncanny. Our feelings confirm Freud's observation that there are many more means of creating uncanny effects in fiction than there are in real life.

Fictional realities such as Luther present special problems for the reader. The sense of the uncanny must be balanced by behavior that is consistent, in some respects, with historical reconstructions. Kleist realizes the necessary balance by giving the fictional presence a voice we have already heard: it is as if a ghost confronts us. Luther, upon seeing Kohlhaas in the room, tells him to leave, for the man is obnoxious: "Your breath is pestilence, your presence ruination." ("Dein Odem ist Pest und deine Nähe Verderben!") When Kohlhaas asks for a pass so that he may go to Dresden, Luther calls him an "impious and terrible man" ("heilloser und entsetzlicher Mann"). And later, Luther calls Kohlhaas a "mad, incomprehensible, and terrible fellow" (124) ("rasender, unbegreiflicher und entsetzlicher Mensch" [46–47]). When Kohlhaas argues that he has been cast out of society and denied the protection of the laws, Luther denies that that is so and adds that Kohlhaas has no right to judge the Junker, for only God can judge.

This is the Luther we know through documents, the Luther that breathes such arrogance and self-righteousness. It is as if our narrative reflects the dialectic of Luther's strange sympathy, then curse, and finally attempt at self-justification that are exhibited in the three pamphlets he wrote on the Peasant Wars. When he belatedly softens the harshness of condemnation expressed in "Against the Robbing and Murdering Hordes of Peasants," he speaks with brutal directness: "A rebel is not worth rational arguments, for he does not accept them. You have to answer people like that with a fist, until the sweat drops off their noses. The peasants would not listen; they would not let anyone tell them anything so their ears must now be unbuttoned with musket balls till their heads jump off their shoulders."[9] A worthy opponent to Kohlhaas, Luther must give in to the demand for justice, for Kohlhaas is in the right. That, too, is consistent with the expectations we have of a religious leader who maintained a sense of justice despite his unsympathetic fulminations against the peasants. The contradictory qualities in his nature, so well represented in the story, help to place Luther on the level of a mythic presence; but unlike traditional mythic characters—Clytemnestra, Oedipus, Medea—Luther is known to us independently of Kleist's story. Kleist preserves the different levels of belief we possess in regard to Luther: "Luther" is really Luther; "Luther" behaves in the manner we have internalized as a set of deep feelings and beliefs about the man; and "Luther" responds to Kohlhaas as the story demands he respond, with both damnation and sympathy. That combination accords with expectations we bring to the story from our reading of history. Merging "Luther" and Luther creates a strong feel-

9. Martin Luther, "An Open Letter on the Harsh Book against the Peasants," in *Luther's Works,* ed. Robert C. Schultz and Helmut T. Lehmann (Philadelphia: 1955), 46:65.

ing of the uncanny, for a fictional-real presence connects the plea for justice addressed to Luther with the mysterious other realm that breaks into the story as it attempts to find justice.

III

Three forces determine the vector of Kohlhaas's fate: his respect for the law, his belief in the Redeemer, and the power given him by the old Gypsy to subdue his enemies through knowledge of the future, which makes him godlike. All three forces, coming to work on behalf of Kohlhaas's fate, are rejected by him in his own peculiar way. Each force by itself might realize freedom for Kohlhaas were he only to accept its conditions, but the conditions required would deny the return of the horses as they originally were. Not even the Gypsy can compel Kohlhaas to use the information on the scrap of paper to gain his freedom, so she bids him good-bye; but before she goes Kohlhaas asks her how she came to possess her powerful *Wissenschaft*, to which she replies that when they again meet, everything he wishes to know will be revealed to him.

That mysterious prophecy strikes us, the readers, as believable because Kohlhaas has recognized in the Gypsy the likeness of his dead wife, Lisbeth. It is from "Lisbeth" that Kohlhaas receives a note just before he goes to the executioner's block, confirming for him and for us that the *Wissenschaft* of the Gypsy is really the knowledge and practice of the moral imperative possessed by the wife to whom Kohlhaas could not listen. That knowledge, now internalized by Kohlhaas, identifies him as one person among the multitudes who could stand alone as the ethical hero, patterned on a Kantian model—surpassing, in fiction, anything Kant could have dreamed.

The likeness of the Gypsy to Lisbeth brings together in the final scene the two forces of feeling that have driven the plot from its beginning: *Rechtsgefühl* and *Entfremdungsgefühl*. Kohlhaas's sense of right made him a robber and a murderer, and it is the same sensibility that leads him to accept his own beheading as fitting payment for the justice of restoration. Justice is done out of strangeness, and in strangeness we find the path to the executioner's block. As the story ends, all about us is familiar, yet all about us is strange, alienated, remote. Neither belief in legal rationality nor faith in divine righteousness would allow us to find an appropriate set of feelings towards Kohlhaas's death. We are left suspended, as if in an equilibrium of forces, with neither sorrow nor exultation, neither contentment nor agitation.

It is precisely this concluding stasis of feeling that makes *Michael Kohlhaas* a rare event, a truly philosophical narrative. That is not because the story was, perhaps, inspired by reflections upon Kantian morality, but rather because Kleist penetrates to the very mystery of justice itself: when justice is done, the world drops away and all feeling is irrelevant. That penetration establishes our story as the very opposite of tragedy as we know it in the classical dramas, tragedy defined in the *Poetics*. Our story possesses all the elements of tragedy, including the powerful presence of the uncanny; yet it is in several ways a negation of tragic elements. This is not to claim that our story is, as it might be popular to say today, an "antitragedy"; it is not that at all, but rather a complement to tragedy, for it resides within the world out of which tragedy is generated—the dimly imagined realm Kant referred to as the "noumenal." If we were to inhabit that world, in which there would be at last a coincidence between aspiration and reality, we would have for our delectation one story illustrative of our condition, a story that would show us where we had come to, from what earlier condition we had come—and that story would be *Michael Kohlhaas*.

But what then of our hero? He possesses all the qualities of the tragic hero: nobility, obduracy, an alliance with strangeness, unrequitable anger, and strangest of all, excessive virtue. Yet his fate is to have justice done to him, and that seems appropriate for one excessively virtuous. Curiously, that is never the fate of the tragic hero of old—the tragic hero before modernity—for whom the justice realized is cosmic, not private. Our hero, in contrast, lives to see justice done him in a private way, for his horses are restored to him. That realization means Kohlhaas has achieved what no tragic hero ever could achieve: he has mended the past.

The past has been reconstituted, and that restoration is the outcome a tragic hero would effect if he could. Kohlhaas violates the boundaries of tragedy and flies in the face of ordinary experience. These violations carry the implication of his quest outside the commonly accepted boundaries of inference and into the postulated noumenal realm underlying tragic action and everyday morality. His steadfastness in the pursuit of justice is rewarded with a restoration that goes beyond even that which he sought, for—and this moves the reader deeper into uncanny possibilities—his beloved wife is brought back to life. The Gypsy, he believes (and we must believe) is the Lisbeth who died. As he goes to his death he is given evidence that the science of the Gypsy has brought back his wife as well as his two horses. The world is as it originally was, and Kohlhaas is no longer its avenging angel.

> POSTSCRIPT
> And the Archangel Michael seized me by the right hand
> And lifted me up and led me forth into all the secrets,
> And he showed me all the secrets of righteousness.
>   1 Enoch 71:3

There is in *Michael Kohlhaas* a remarkable interweaving of history and vision. The history represents a period of intense temporal and spiritual conflict in the midst of which Martin Luther now seems to have been a dominant force and interpreter. The vision is continuous with the history in that it takes freely from the messianic fervor that characterized the time and that we know from the apocryphal books excluded from the Hebrew Bible. Our story has about it something of the apocryphal tone, for it stands outside all the traditional plots in both classical tragedy and romantic pathos. It allies itself with that "middle" part of the Bible so worrisome to Melville's Confidence Man, which I will discuss in the next chapter.

The kingdom of *Michael Kohlhaas* is that of the modern legally ordered state; its eschatological vision—if I may call it that—is of a justice beyond anything law can deliver. One of the strange aspects of the story is that its vision is more philosophical than religious. It has its closest analogue in the unified reality that the philosopher Kant insisted underlies the human search for a moral order. In that unified reality, one's aspirations to justice exactly coincide with the values of the universe. If that is the sudden coherence realized by Michael Kohlhaas just before he dies, then we may understand the stasis of feeling and belief that overcomes us as we conclude our reading. The story forces upon us a kind of philosophical regression, for it affirms with its demonstration one of our deepest wishes that we would believe above all others: that the universe is just, that justice *can* be done.

6 Contradiction and Repression: Paradox and Mask in American Tragedy

Contradiction and repression are concepts whose conjunction may seem odd, yet they are related in ways that give a basic structure to narrative and lead us to the inner reality of tragedy as it shapes language and character. Contradiction is a logical and philosophical concept wider in significance than has been recognized in recent logical thought; repression is a psychoanalytic concept originally developed to explain clinical interpretations, and we now recognize it to have application in the arts. The two, when regarded in the context of a theory of the linguistic arts (which I take to include philosophical writing) and in particular of tragedy, reinforce one another in our interpretative efforts.

Strategies for resolving the contradictions of paradox have been a traditional preoccupation of philosophers; from the earliest inquiries into argument, the inborn capacity of language to talk about itself, and therefore to generate paradox, has provided test cases for logical consistency. From Greek speculation we have inherited a whole set of paradoxes, the most famous that of the lying Cretan which generates the "paradox of the liar." How fascinating and puzzling the paradox: it appears over and over again, in philosophy, scripture, and commentaries right through to the present. And now, with the logical theories of modernity, it takes on new life, draws the logician's attention to a "solution," and generates further logical difficulties. The lying Cretan indeed! How odd that a wiley islander should confound Athenian sophisticates—and on the ground where the tragic riddle was a common presence. Perhaps that is why the paradox of the liar met with such intense interest in Athens, where tragic plots came into being, each posing a paradoxical problem for which there was no final logical determination. Or, put another way, both logical paradox and tragic riddle reveal a disquieting aspect of language: that there are many sentences whose truth cannot be determined. There is another interconnection between paradox and riddle: tragic riddles are accompanied by masks.

Paradox has its counterpart in the mask as an instrument of expressive action, and the mask itself, like paradox, takes many different forms in various cultural traditions. Paradox and mask are the manifest evidences of deep inner conditions of contradiction and repression.

The paradox of the liar has held millennial attention because it reveals to us an aspect of language we would rather deny and escape—the indeterminacy of truth-value. The mask, a universal artifact with a variety of uses, represents an aspect of our human selves that disrupts community and throws moral constancy into doubt, therefore implying indeterminacy of character. The paradox of the liar may be resolved, it is claimed, through analyses that assign truth-values to sentences, though that solution still misses some of the difficulties of paradox; and the mask can be stripped off to reveal the identity of the wearer, though that, too, misses the complexities of character indeterminacy.

We can think of the paradox of the liar as a linguistic mask that conceals the true meaning of the utterance of the speaker; and we can think of the mask as a paradox which conceals or prevents our establishing the identity of the person. Underneath these symptoms—for so I conceive paradox and mask—there are conditions of language and character that make determinate resolution difficult, perhaps impossible. In the case of language, speakers maintain simultaneously contradictory propositions; in the case of persons, identity hides behind repression. Psychologically we are contradictory persons; logically we are masking speakers.

Of all the linguistic enactments, tragic drama most explicitly relies upon and explores the riddles of paradox and mask. Tragedy, in its use of paradox and mask, demonstrates the difficulty—perhaps the impossibility—of resolving the central mystery of utterance and character. It offers cases of indeterminacy of meaning and of character that will not yield to any "solution," or "explanation." Yet that conclusion, so clearly exhibited by tragedy, generates philosophical unease, since philosophy takes pride in the resolution of contradiction and paradox and since philosophers become skittish in the presence of the psychoanalytic concept of repression. Philosophy prefers clear, truth-determined sentences and transparent, action-accountable persons. It is not in philosophy that the unresolved riddle resides—yet there, too, it resides!

It is not in philosophy, whose every effort is to resolve indeterminacy, that we can study indeterminacy; rather, it is in tragedy and the novel that we find the stamina to confront, to explore, and to tolerate indeterminacy. My concern in this chapter is to examine contradiction and repression with their attendant symptoms, paradox and mask, and to look at one instance of the New World novel in which paradox and mask are set in the very center of its expression. Tragic action and tragic character here receive an interpretation far removed from their manifest origins in Old World cultures, and tragedy sinks down almost to oblivion under the repression of American optimism.

My procedure here will be to analyze the ways in which contradiction and repression work in a set of paradoxes generated by a novel, *The Confidence Man*, by Herman Melville. I choose that book because within it the logical and psychological strategies of contradiction and repression in a repressed tragic setting are closely examined. *The Confidence Man* demonstrates the ways in which the two structures interinanimate one another in a cultural tradition that sets a high value on the determination of truth and falsity in narrative representation. Because philosophy grew up side by side with narrative fiction, the conflicts of determinacy and indeterminacy of truth-value were entertained in the earliest arguments we possess. It has often been pointed out that early poets, particularly Pindar (see *Nemea* 7), make the question of truth a central concern of poetry, as Plato does in his celebration of the conflict between the truth of poetry and the truth of philosophy.

Herman Melville, in *The Confidence Man*, reiterated an old riddle in the New World. In the tragedy of American frontier life he saw the question of a solution posed afresh: can the old riddles be solved if we believe that humankind can be granted a new beginning? Perhaps the waters of the Mississippi could cleanse New World explorers of Old World bafflements.

I

A basic discovery in the logic of discourse was the familiar paradox of the lair. In its simplest form it is the recognition that "All Cretans are liars" is a sentence that, when uttered by a Cretan, must be false if true and true if false. The undecidability of truth and falsehood as properties of sentences has since the earliest recorded logical inquiries been seen as a puzzle and a tribulation. Recurrent modern analyses establish once more the importance of the problem and, perhaps, the impotence of philosophers in the face of the difficulties surrounding indeterminacy of meaning. Perplexity persists; paradox, meanwhile, has received two modern treatments that will be helpful in shifting the focus from enactments of philosophy to enactments of narrative fiction as they continue their millennial disputes.

In his discussion of the object-language in chapter 4 of *An Inquiry into Meaning and Truth*, Bertrand Russell argued that in order to avoid or escape the paradox of the liar, we must introduce into language the idea of a "hierarchy of languages," for without that concept we cannot understand how to use terms such as "true" and "false."[1] If we ask of particular assertions, claims, and descriptions, "Are these sentences true or false?" we cannot understand the answer given in some cases unless we understand and use the structure of a hierarchy of languages. Thus, if I assert, "I am telling a lie of order n," I am telling a lie, to be sure, but a lie of order n + 1. For to say that a sentence I utter is a lie, I must be able to talk about that sentence by means of other sen-

1. Bertrand Russell, *An Inquiry into Meaning and Truth* (London: George Allen and Unwin, 1940).

tences whose standing in the hierarchy of languages is "above" the sentence I uttered. When I say, "I am lying," that sentence is *about* the sentence I have already uttered. If the sentence I uttered is exactly the sentence, "I am lying," then I am generating the paradox of the liar, but at the same time resolving the paradox insofar as I understand that what I am doing is talking *about* sentences.

"The hierarchy," Russell wrote, "must extend upwards indefinitely, but not downwards, since if it did, language could never get started. There must, therefore, be a language of lowest type." Russell called this "the object-language," or "the primary language."[2]

When we look at the object-language that all discourse presupposes, we must include in it the basic, or primary, language for tragic narrative that I have been considering. In novels (such as *The Confidence Man*), just as in the language of everyday speech and in the symbolic languages of sophisticated philosophical analyses of language, there is a base from which the levels of language rise. But as soon as that is said, a problem obtrudes: in the case of both natural, everyday language and literary narrative languages, there seems to be an obverse hierarchy, if I may call it that—a hierarchy *downwards*. I am referring to the common idea that there are sentences—hidden and latent meanings— that, if we pursue the spatial metaphor, are under, or below, or somehow depend from, the given sentences. We assume that there are hierarchies in the service of truth/falsehood, the upward-moving hierarchies; and there are hierarchies in the service of meaning, the downward-moving hierarchies. It appears to me now that the way we think about sentences, their meanings, and their truth conditions is in terms of a double pyramid with the apexes joined at the sentence in question, the sentence we are concerned to interpret.

The upper inverted pyramid diagrams the linguistic levels made up of sentences about the sentences below them in the hierarchy; if one sentence suggests or expresses a contradiction, the next sentence above it may resolve the contradiction.

The lower pyramid diagrams the *interpretative* relationships of sentences. Each sentence receives interpretative explication by and through the sentence standing below it.

2. Ibid., 63.

The upper pyramid, concerned with the obstacles to assigning truth-values to sentences, helps the reader or hearer to overcome the indeterminacy of meaning generated by the linguistic conditions that allow a sentence to make a claim: the sentence is true, or the sentence is false. And the possibility is always present that the sentence falls into indeterminancy of truth-value.

The lower pyramid, concerned with indeterminacy of meaning generated by repression, establishes conditions whereby indeterminacy may be overcome, that is, by lifting repression. The indeterminacy of incompleteness of meaning can be overcome if that which is repressed is brought into consciousness. With enlarged consciousness, indeterminacy may be erased, just as it may in the upper pyramid with explicit relationships of sentences referring to other sentences. Indeterminacies of truth-value and indeterminacies of meaning plague the readers of literary texts, and strategies for assigning truth and meaning to sentences of a text are goals of literary interpretation.

The concepts of contradiction and repression have been investigated in two quite distinct traditions, in both of which indeterminacy of meaning was one of the problems to be solved. It was clear to both Bertrand Russell and Sigmund Freud that indeterminacy of meaning obstructed the analysis of language, upon which philosophical and psychological theories depend. It is helpful, therefore, to consider the methods they relied upon to clarify the source of, and achieve a cure for, indeterminacy of meaning.

Russell attacks the problem of indeterminacy first through the construction of a hierarchy of language, and he uses that to demonstrate a basic linguistic reality, namely, that we use language to talk about itself in such a way that when we ask if a sentence is true or false, we are talking about that sentence by means of a sentence of a second order of reference—that is to say, the second order talks about and refers to the first order. Having established that, Russell goes on to make a second logical observation that is at the same time a psychological observation; it has to do with denoting terms, especially the terms "nothing," "something," and "everything."

Russell's observations upon the three denoting terms are helpful to our understanding of fictional narrations and their sentences. First, Russell's way of looking at denoting terms ("nothing," "something," and "everything") establishes a relationship among them. To bring them into logical transparency, he proposes that we take as basic those sentences the truths of which are affirmed, for both logically and psychologically we commit ourselves to sentences that are presumed to be true. If we take true sentences as basic, then we begin our linguistic connection to the world with the basic term "everything." The terms "nothing" and "something" are to be defined in terms of "everything."

Russell proposes the following interpretations. To be able to use the term "nothing" correctly, I must understand that "'X is false' is always true"; and to use the denoting term "something," I must understand that "It is false that 'X is false' is always true." I want to emphasize the psychological implications of this interpretation: the predicate "is true" is given logical primacy because of a psychological disposition, namely, that we stand to experience as affirming beings; that we presume, in our relations to the world, that certain events *are* happening, certain conditions *are* realized; and that we use negation as dependent upon an initial basic affirmation. Thus the logical clarity Russell seeks turns out to be an expression of a psychological disposition of human beings.

Russell's analysis of denoting terms might at first appear to be very like Freud's analysis of negation. Psychoanalytic theory argues for affirmation as basic and negation as parasitic upon affirmation. At first we might think that psychologically Russell and Freud agree; but the seeming agreement—due in part to Freud's taking over the general Weltanschauung of science (as he himself put it)—disappears upon closer inspection. In two respects Freud's view of negation and its functions differs from Russell's. First, Freud found in clinical experience that the use of negation as such frequently masks or serves as a substitute formation for affirmation. Where negation appears, Freud cautions, suspect affirmation. For Freud, negation is a symptom as well as a sign. Where negation occurs there may well be repression; the very use of negation requires interpretation, for it can serve as a clue to a developing condition, that a repression can be lifted.

Second, and more difficult to explicate, Freud's description of cases in which negation has to be interpreted by the analyst makes use of the concept of "primary-process thinking." In that process—contrasted with "secondary-process thinking," in which sentences observing the rules of logic are the mode of articulation—unconscious mental processes employ images rather than words. Freud, in these explorations, is setting up the interpretative moves downwards that I see as the counterpart to Russell's moves upwards.

Here is the way Russell states the case for the upwards hierarchy: "Denial presupposes a form of words, and proceeds to state that this form of words is false. The word 'not' is only significant when attached to a sentence, and therefore presupposes language. Consequently, if 'p' is a sentence of the primary language, 'not-p' is a sentence of the secondary language."[3]

While this description suggests a psychological structure in accord with the psychoanalytic conception of negation, the logical analysis is directed to secondary-process thought only. In contrast, the analysis in the clinic and in psychoanalytic interpretative strategies concentrates on negation as expressed in nonverbal as well as verbal forms. Visual images, dreams, and fantasies express negation in primary-process thinking; so that negation, Freud maintains, is to be found in a variety of representations. Thus while Russell would remove the roots of paradox by clearing the ground of contradiction, Freud would maintain that in the primary process there is no clearly established, identifiable construction that could be called, in the logical sense, a contradiction. As Freud states it, "Exemption from mutual contradiction is a characteristic of the system Ucs."

But the two views of negation share a concern: both realize that for the individual, coming to understand and use the term "not" is critical to stages of maturation. Learning to use "not" is a part of growing up.

Although Russell did not pursue the developmental aspect of language use, recent studies in logical theory have added to Russell's notion of hierarchy a developmental component, to deal with the achievement of growing up in language.

Saul Kripke, in a paper entitled "Outline of a Theory of Truth," writes, "*Many, probably most, of our ordinary assertions about truth and falsity are liable, if the empirical facts are extremely unfavorable,*

---

3. Ibid., Chap. 4.

to exhibit paradoxical features."[4] Kripke's awareness of the unfavorable empirical facts leads him to suggest a developmental thesis in regard to the ways we learn to use language. Our capacity to use the predicates "is true" and "is false" matures slowly: "The sense in which we can say, in natural language, that a Liar sentence is not true must be thought of as associated with some later stage in the development of natural language, one in which speakers reflect on the generation process leading to the minimal fixed point." What Kripke means is that our language, in its everyday use, has built-in limitations, and that we learn their nature and scope as we grow up. Philosophy makes discoveries about language as philosophy itself matures. One of the things philosophy of language has come to apprehend is this: "There are assertions we can make about the object language which we cannot make in the object language. For example, Liar sentences are *not true* in the object language, in the sense that the inductive process never makes them true; but we are precluded from saying this in the object language by our interpretation of negation and the truth predicate."[5]

The logical model of language I proposed earlier, derived from Russell's idea of hierarchy upwards, now is expanded to include a developmental aspect that relates the logic of predicates to the logic of psychoanalytic distinctions. Kripke's description of learning to use the word "true" establishes the connection:

> Suppose we are explaining the word "true" to someone who does not understand it. We may say that we are entitled to assert (or deny) of any sentence that it is true precisely under the circumstances when we can assert (or deny) the sentence itself. Our interlocutor then can understand what it means, say, to attribute truth to "snow is white" but will still be puzzled about attributions of truth to sentences containing the word "true" itself. Since he did not understand these sentences initially, it will be equally nonexplanatory, initially, to explain to him that to call such a sentence "true"

4. Saul Kripke, "Outline of a Theory of Truth," *The Journal of Philosophy* 72 (1975): 691. Italics in original.
5. Ibid., 714.

("false") is tantamount to asserting (denying) the sentence itself.[6]

Kripke, in explaining the underlying developmental process presup-
posed by the stages through which an initiate passes in learning not
only the use of language, but the ways in which language talks about
itself, describes the process of mastery: "In this manner, the subject
will eventually be able to attribute truth to more and more statements
involving the notion of truth itself."[7]

In story-telling discourse, just as in everyday language, we encounter a great range of statements "involving the notion of truth itself."
Our experience with them as narrative strategies encourages a system-
atic exploration of how truth and statements involving truth are to be
interpreted. I shall study this phase of cultural development in my
analysis of *The Confidence Man.* Because of the philosophical preoccupation with the concept of truth, modernity has become intensely
aware of the capacity within language to think about language. The
philosophical inquiry carried on by Russell and Kripke is supplemented
by the psychoanalytic model of primary-process thought. Of course,
the concept of the primary process cannot stand alone, but is interwoven with the concept of repression and, especially, interpretation. It
was in *The Interpretation of Dreams* that Freud demonstrated the
method of interpretation in moving back and forth from latent to manifest, from primary process to secondary process. To complement the
logical model of how the use of "is true" ought to be interpreted, I turn
now to the psychoanalytic model. The two together allow the reader of
enactments to resolve paradox and to penetrate mask.

II

Language is utterance; mask is visage. Out of the mouth
comes language, shaped by the face. Interpretation of utterance begins
with the initial encounter: sounds shaped, words sounded, notes
struck; facial expression, physiognomic details, overall countenance—
all yield initial clues to meaning. But whether or not the face lies cannot be determined by the sentences it utters; whether the sentences are

6. Ibid., 701.
7. Ibid.

true or false cannot be judged by the visage alone. An interpretation is formed by the hearer-seer of language and face. Interpretations entertain belief: "The sentences of the utterance are true/false; the evidence of the face is the self/mask."

But when the "speaker" is a text for which the living storyteller is gone, where there is no note sounded in the air and no face from which the sentences emerge, then the sentences organized into story create a presence, give life to inert separate elements whose quickening depends upon the inspired breath of the reader or hearer. Where the sentences produce paradox, truth hides; where character is masked, person becomes elusive, sometimes ephemeral, even evanescent. Where there is paradox, suspect mask; where there is mask, search for the paradox it conceals.

What has our cultural tradition given us that will guide us in listening to and understanding stories? Philosophers, now as in the past, shy away from the problem, preferring to stay within the circle drawn by Russell's examples. Paradox requires a hierarchical analysis, raising language to new levels; but the mask of speaking remains impenetrable. Issues of "truth" in stories never correspond to the issues raised in natural language use. Story calls upon us to plumb depths, to move downwards into the hierarchy of meaning that opens itself to interpretation. And the way downwards is blocked not only by the mythic guardian monsters barring the way to the underworld, but by the simple, human mechanism of repression—a powerful obstruction.

It is to clinical investigations, rather than logical ones, that we must turn for guidance. Among the discoveries Freud made in the study of negation is this: "The content of a repressed image or idea can make its way into consciousness, on condition that it is *negated*. Negation is a way of taking cognizance of what is repressed; indeed it is already a lifting of the repression, though not, of course, an acceptance of what is repressed."[8] This observation and the suggested explanation of the function of negation can be applied to linguistic enactments, both written and oral. There is in linguistic art, as there is in the person, repressed, latent, hidden, material waiting to be interpreted. The parallel between clinical inquiry and the reader or hearer's interpretation of

8. Freud, "Negation," in *Std. Ed.*, 19:235–36.

story makes the psychoanalytic method applicable to narrative enactments.

In the clinic, repression is thought of as one of the vicissitudes suffered by an instinctual impulse or demand; when the impulse or demand comes into conflict with others—either external or internal in origin—it may be pushed out of consciousness, or never allowed into consciousness. That is to say, in Freud's conceptualization, the ideational representative of the instinct cannot be entertained consciously. But the instinct continues to exist as a force and a psychic reality, however strongly denied. In the clinic, the evidence for repression is complex; it includes symptoms of a neurotic and of a psychotic kind, evidence from dreams, language of the clinical exchange, and bodily gestures.

In linguistic art the vicissitudes of repression are symptomatically identified by paradox and by masking, the two common means I shall examine here. The contradictions generated by paradox and mask stand as evidence of repression, which keeps dangerous, threatening wishes, beliefs, and thoughts out of the manifest content of the narrative. And where such thoughts are denied—where there is negation—the reader or hearer should suspect a step is being taken towards the lifting of repression.

As Freud recognized, violation of the law of contradiction has psychological as well as logical consequences. Both Russell and Kripke make clear in their strategies of interpretation—though they do not pay conscious attention to the psychological—that the resolution of the liar's paradox has consequences for our beliefs about the world. Of course they point out, as Freud does, the unacceptability of contradiction: for the logician, it is a violation of a basic "law" of logic; for the psychologist, it is a basic violation of secondary-process thinking, which accepts and works within the "laws" of logic. For the psychologist, a way must be found to overcome the violation and still preserve its full meaning. Thus Freud's means of resolution have a central role in the interpretation of narrative fiction, where "resolution" means something like "expansion and full preservation of meaning." Interpretative strategies in the psychoanalytic domain are like those that Hegel worked out for the philosophical interpretation of history and culture: each stage of interpretation preserves, protects, and makes coherent the earlier ones, so that an *expansion* of meaning is achieved. Therefore, the psychoanalytic method attempts to open up the ways enactments work in their pursuit of truth. Fictional narration, drama, and all the other linguistic forms of enactment have developed their own means to cope with paradox and negation, and those means are well described by the psychoanalytic strategies for coping with repression.

One way in which repressed material becomes conscious is through displacement, for consciousness can tolerate repressed material if it is removed sufficiently from the force that causes repression. Freud describes the possibility of the appearance of the repressed:

> Let us make it clear that it is not even correct to suppose that repression withholds from the conscious *all* the derivatives of what was primarily repressed. If these derivatives have become sufficiently far removed from the repressed representative, whether owing to the adoption of distortion or by reason of the number of intermediate links inserted, they have free access to the conscious. It is as though the resistance of the conscious against them was a function of their distance from what was originally repressed.[9]

Extending Freud's concept of repression—and the ways around repression—to the mask, I suggest that masking is a gestural and physiognomic means to deal with repression. Masking performs two functions: it allows ideational and affective material to get into consciousness through displacement; and at the same time, masking conceals, hides, keeps the dangerous, threatening thoughts out of consciousness. The mask represents both the material secondary process may work with and the primary-process imagistic representation of the instinctual.

Paradox and mask appear frequently in fictional narration, and to that I now turn.

When a paradox, such as the liar's paradox, appears in fictional narration, the indeterminacy on the level of secondary-process thought— where the truth conditions of the statements are obscure—initiates the

9. Freud, "Repression," in *Std. Ed.*, 14:149.

lifting of the repressed primary-process thought. Indeterminacy, which is psychologically generated by denial (the use of "not"), can be generated in narrative fiction by a simple contradiction, even an obscurity, as well as by denial. But in the case of fiction, the *logician's* technique of resolution does not clear away indeterminacy. Hierarchical separation of "p" and "not-p" works in logically controlled secondary thought, but does not work in cases where both secondary and primary thought are expressed. In fictional narration, resolution of contradiction and lifting of obscurity are achieved through allowing repressed meaning to emerge. In this process a mask is removed.

Fictional narration has at its command a number of means to create paradox and masking; I shall examine one—embeddedness, the condition in which one story encloses another story so that a hierarchy of stories is established. This is a venerable strategy of linguistic enactment, powerfully worked in the novel; it can be seen, though, in a variety of genres, for example, the *Symposium, The Decameron,* and *The Confidence Man.* I shall turn now to Melville's novel, where paradox and masking display their power to reveal repressed meaning and, in the process, to remove indeterminacy of meaning.

III

The opening chapter of Melville's *The Confidence Man,* a novel completed in 1857 and the last he published, presents the reader with an unusual paradox. A man described as "dressed in cream colors" and wearing a "white fur hat" with "a long fleecy nap" writes upon a slate a set of sentences that turn out to be quotations from First Corinthians, chapter 13. "Charity thinketh no evil," he writes; "Charity suffereth long and is kind"; and so on through the sentences St. Paul so dramatically wrote to the congregation awaiting his visit. The crowd watching realizes that the writer is a mute evangelist; he presents them, and us the readers, with sentences taken from another book.

The writer of the sentences is dressed as if in sheep's clothing, and therefore we might think he is one of the false prophets Jesus warned about in the Sermon on the Mount. However, the possible false prophet might just as well be described as "the Lamb" and therefore would be the departed Christ; if so, we are hearing Jesus preach the words of Paul.[10]

Since his affinities to the spiritual realm are indeterminate, the writer of the sentences offers us, as readers, two possibilities: he is a false prophet, and thus what he wrote—the sentences set into quotation marks by the novelist—are false; or he is indeed the returned Christ, usurping the teaching that best conveys his spiritual message. If he is the false prophet, what he writes is true if false and false if true, and the reader is entangled in the familiar liar's paradox. However, since the sentences are quoted in a fictional narration and all the sentences can be declared "fictions," the truth conditions applying to the sentences become more deeply indeterminate than those of the sentence originally uttered by the Cretan and his representations in the logic books. (Though we might ponder the question: are logic texts fictional?)

If the writer is indeed the Lamb, then the indeterminacy rests on an identification of the character as the returned Christ, and that identification also remains indeterminate because all the characters in the novel wear masks. It is even possible that the central speaker in each episode is yet another masked representation of one character, the Confidence Man.[11] We are abandoned to a limbo of indeterminacy, a limbo of paradox and mask generated by contradiction and repression. To escape the indeterminacy, we must somehow, as we read, determine the foundational affirmations in the text by resorting to the upwards and downwards hierarchies of truth-value and meaning.

The paradox of the liar is generated by the scene in which the mute writes sentences upon a slate; yet, as we read, we discover that there is another indeterminacy, that of character—namely, the identity of the writer of the sentences. Hence there is a second paradox here, one we are familiar with from our knowledge of classical tragedy—a paradox

10. "Beware of false prophets, which come to you in sheep's clothing, but inwardly they are ravening wolves." Matt. 7:15.

11. There is also a paradox of quotation here, or at least an indeterminacy of quotation. The Mute writes on the slate; the quotation marks in the text may be there as an orthographic convention because the text is reporting that the sentences are utterances, for which we conventionally use quotation marks. Or the use may simply indicate that the sentences are from the text of First Corinthians.

of character. We are confronted in this instance, as in the case of tragic drama, with possible contradictions in both *assertion* and *action*. In moving to solve one paradox we are thrust into the other. As we move up the hierarchy of languages to talk *about* the sentences written on the slate, we are yet unable to attach a specific level of language to the writer who produced the sentences. In the textbook case of the Cretan, it has apparently always been assumed we know who the Cretan is: he is a Cretan, or my friend John the Cretan. But in *The Confidence Man* we do not know who speaks, and as we move deeper into the novel, identification of character becomes the overriding concern: we must solve the problem of character indeterminacy before we can resolve the liar's paradox.

Paradox of character, that is, the repression realized through masking, is exhibited throughout the plot; it comes to rest in its most complicate inner design and mystery in the center of the book. (I shall later recall this centrality as a reflection of the novel's description of the way the Bible is put together, with the Apocrypha in the middle.) There we are led downwards through the inverted hierarchy of meaning, each new level at once an unmasking and the discovery of yet another mask. I shall go a little way towards unmasking.

In the center of the novel, five levels of embeddedness can be distinguished.[12]

(1) A character introduced as "the Cosmopolitan" (whom I take to be the Confidence Man in one of his masquerades) meets a character referred to simply as "the Westerner," who in turn refers to a "Colonel Moredock," the Indian Hater. That the Confidence Man in his many masks is a deceiver we are well aware; and in this episode he is confronted with the Westerner, whose false teeth are "too good to be true." (2) Colonel Moredock is described by the Westerner (who may have caught a glimpse of Moredock asleep) as silky-bearded, curly-headed, "juicy as a peach," and oddly, sleeping beneath a set of deer antlers. The description puts Moredock in the class of fertility gods. I say this because Moredock combines the qualities of the Dionysus we know from Euripides' *Bacchae* with the dress we know from American

12. Herman Melville, *The Confidence Man* (New York: New American Library, 1954), 151–67.

Indian ceremonials. (3) The story of Moredock comes from the lips of Judge Hall, from whom the Westerner has heard and *exactly* memorized the telling. Judge Hall describes the nature of the Indian Hater in a disquisition entitled "The Metaphysics of Indian Hating." And in order to exemplify the beliefs and behavior of Moredock, Judge Hall relates a second story embedded in the first. (4) Judge Hall's second story concerns the little settlement of Wrights and Weavers, who make a pact with their Indian enemy, Mocmohoc. He invites them to a meal and slays them all. When asked why he broke the covenant, Mocmohoc laughs: it was they who broke the covenant, for they trusted Mocmohoc. And that trust itself is a betrayal. (5) The next story concerns the actual life experience of Moredock, who is described, despite his dedication to killing Indians, as having "at bottom a loving heart." All Indian haters are so characterized by Judge Hall, for they are all, like Moredock, men of love. This characterization is challenged by the Cosmopolitan, who takes the odd contradiction—Moredock is a man of hate and he is a man of love—as a betrayal of the basic human fellow feeling: *trust*.

The metaphysics of Indian hating—truly a philosophical subject—is the central theme in the nest of stories. It presents a series of paradoxes: paradoxes of truth, of meaning, of affect, of character. How can the paradoxes be resolved?

The very title of the chapter, "Containing the Metaphysics of Indian-Hating, According to the Views of One Evidently Not So Prepossessed as Rousseau in Favor of Savages" (chapter 26 of *The Confidence Man*), presents a series of overlapping masks whose configuration and obscuration it is the reader's task to recognize and penetrate. Melville here is satirically presenting the teachings of two popular writers. Rousseau's views on savages are themselves paradoxical, for the early "natural" condition of man is at once defended in theory and denied in the life of Rousseau himself. And we know that a later philosopher, Schopenhauer—also a thinker of many masks—dared address his readers, for whom he had deep contempt, on "The Metaphysics of the Love of the Sexes," in one title both affirming and denying the tradition of repression that surrounds sex. The mythic figure of Moredock in this philosophical company, paired as he is with the savage Mocmohoc, occupies the center of *The Confidence Man* with a challenge to received beliefs on morality, religion, and philosophy itself. Through the masks of Rousseau and Schopenhauer speak the enemies of man, themselves men: *homo homini lupus*, a phrase quoted by Schopenhauer in chapter 47 of *The World as Will and Idea* and repeated by Melville in the opening chapter of *The Confidence Man*. Moredock and Mocmohoc, sharing between them this slyly referred to narrative reality, generate paradoxes of character and action whose resolution initiates the lifting of repression. Through denial we are able to entertain heterodox beliefs. Consciousness is deepened by the move downwards through the levels of embedded stories and their images.

The story most deeply embedded is that of Mocmohoc and his "betrayal" of the Wrights and Weavers, of whom he says, when reproached for his treachery: "Treachery? pale face! 'Twas they who broke the covenant first, in coming all together; they broke it first in trusting Mocmohoc." How are we readers to understand this claim? Our attention must center first on the "covenant," an odd word to use here, related to the biblical covenant and the ways in which it was broken.

For a Christian community to break its covenant with God, it is enough to put trust in a savage, in a representative of those satanic forces against which the followers of the true God are arrayed. Simply by making a covenant with a savage, the Christian settlers free the savage from any obligation because his adversaries have violated their first covenant. From the Christian fundamental point of view, the settlers are in the wrong, for they have cast off their God to embrace the representative of satanic presence. The devil knows this, and true to the nature of the Evil One, he exercises his wickedness.

We, as readers, are expected to know this, too. We are therefore led to raise this knowledge up to the level of the next surrounding story, that of Moredock. Once we apply the knowledge and insight gained from the innermost story to the story next in the hierarchy, we are in a position to "solve" the paradox of character, that is, the seeming contradiction in Moredock's being both a man of hate and a man of love. But a solution here requires more than a logical analysis; it calls upon the reader to discover the repressed and so far unavailable part of the text. It is the unavailable elements that render the story indeterminate.

Moredock can be described as a man of hate and a man of love because he has honored his obligations to the supernatural by keeping the
covenant with God and dedicating his actions to the extirpation of evil.
We readers should understand that he lives according to Christian principles. What, then, are we to think of Christianity? Our reading forces
us to regard Christianity and its teachings with a new, critical detachment and to entertain the thought, now brought into consciousness,
that the doctrines of American religious fundamentalism are in-
humane.

Taking this awareness up yet one more level, we arrive at the description of Moredock with which the narration began:

> The colonel was at that moment sleeping on wolf-skins
> in the corn loft above, so we must not talk very loud, for
> the colonel had been out all night hunting (Indians,
> mind), and it would be cruel to disturb his sleep. Curious
> to see one so famous, we waited two hours over, in the
> hope he would come forth; but he did not. . . . while
> my father was watering the horses, I slipped back into
> the cabin. . . . in the further corner I saw what I took to
> be the wolf-skins, and on them a bundle of something,
> like a drift of leaves; and at the other end, what seemed
> like a moss-ball; and over it, deer-antlers branched; and
> close by, a small squirrel sprang out from a maple-bowl
> of nuts, brushed the moss-ball with his tail, through a
> hole, and vanished squeaking. That bit of woodland
> scene was all I saw. No Colonel Moredock there unless
> that moss-ball was his curly head, seen in the back
> view. [13]

Moredock appears to be a fertility figure, something like a Dionysus,
vegetation god, or woodland sprite. The branching deer antlers are associated with the spirits of the woodland, and Moredock's close affinity
to nature is made clear by his "body," made up of moss and leaves. If
that *is* the sleeping Indian Hater, then he has a dual nature: part
avenger for the first violation, the revolt against God; and part pagan
force whose origin is in the natural forest world of the Indian. He him-

---

13. Ibid., 149.

self participates in and is himself an aspect of that primitivism the Indian exemplifies, so the deepest nature of Moredock is one with the savage.

Moredock's dedication to Indian killing is analogous to St. Paul's conversion from Judaism to Christianity: St. Paul betrayed his own beliefs and his own people to serve a foreign god, to turn then in the name of that God upon those with whom he lived and from whom he drew his spiritual sustenance. This "conversion" and breaking of a covenant constitutes the deepest betrayal, and it is through such betrayals that the Christian God gains supporters and violent defenders.

Moredock, then, is another appearance—now more difficult to recognize and to admit—of the paradox-asserting mute who wrote the words of St. Paul on the slate. He is also the Dionysian man-beast who poisons and cures, who destroys and loves. He is the very spirit out of which tragic action and tragic understanding arise. Moredock propounds paradox of truth, of character, of affect; and Moredock wears many masks. The very name "Moredock" hides a peculiar meaning through associations that would be known to a writer close to the American wilds: the family of the yellow dock and related plants are used as purgatives to induce vomiting. Moredock carries a name that expresses the revulsion we feel towards his person and his actions, the revulsion of the most vigorous act of rejection we can manifest. Moredock, like the Mute, is dedicated to deep deception, deception we can penetrate only if we allow repressed material having to do with character and action to be brought into consciousness. Resolution of the liar's paradox is only the first step, a step upwards, towards the ultimate steps downwards we must take to penetrate the meaning of the story. Long traditions of philosophical and religious beliefs must be challenged and critically evaluated if we are to open a path from primary-process images to secondary-process articulation of conscious meaning.

Organizations of embeddedness are common throughout stories, story cycles, collections, and traditions of enactments. *The Confidence Man* reaches deeply into unconscious beliefs and affects through a series of tales created out of a particular—and to us transitional—cultural object, the story of the Indian and the Christian settlers. But that is a relevance of the historical background out of which Melville creates a cultural object that in itself creates a consciousness of all those fierce conflicts in philosophy and religion and exemplifies the American effort to rewrite the tradition, to begin afresh. How else could that be done, save through contradiction and repression?

IV

Western philosophy has struggled with the paradoxes of truth, of belief, and of action since the earliest realization that utterances, evidence of the senses, and conduct do not readily exhibit their truth-values. The logical methods of modernity, a development of modern science and mathematics, confidently attack the paradoxes, evincing the superior prowess of modern thought. Constructions in language such as those proposed by Russell put the liar in his place; he cannot mislead with his indeterminacy as long as we keep one rung above him; and it does make one feel secure to know there is a defense against the lying Cretan! But that security is short-lived when one leaves the protected domain of linguistic analysis to wander in the world of tragic awareness and to observe the actions of tragic characters. There, it is as if we join the crowd on the steamboat *Fidèle* to travel down the Mississippi. There, we are helpless without psychology.

A psychological attack on contradiction and repression leads in the other direction, downwards into primary-process thought, where images and words inter-inanimate one another and poetic metaphor emerges. But the two strategic approaches—that of logic and that of psychology—reinforce and enlighten one another. Logical resolution of the paradox of the liar clears the pathway to the lifting of repression. Only after we have read the Mute's sentences and have been forced to come to terms with their indeterminacy are we ready for the deeper contradictions of the story of Moredock. But as we complete our descent into the repressed thought underlying the contradictions of the mute and of Moredock, we are led to the final contradiction *The Confidence Man* forces upon us, and this challenges the whole of the tradition itself.

How are we to read *The Confidence Man* in its relationship to other books? We are beset by books in this book: the Bible, classical writings, and the contemporary transcendentalist preachings are all recalled, commented on, and criticized. It appears now, as we survey the work as a whole, that the book we hold and read stands in a peculiar relationship to its predecessors, the inherited accumulation of "believable," "truthful" books that it contradicts. All texts are thrown into indeterminacy by this text. All books lose their identity before the many masks of *The Confidence Man*. As we read we are tested; as we interpret we are thrown into doubt as to meaning; as we seek comfort and enlightenment we assume a posture of doubting that slowly overwhelms our capacity to make discriminations. There comes to take the place of delight in books an anxiety or phobia towards books. Every text referred to is thrown into doubt. And we are thrown into the thrashing machine of truth, whose sweep across the millennia has cleared the ground of all texts. None remain.

Uncertainty and insecurity replace settled belief and trust in the books of our inheritance, and we are led to make denials. Our denials in turn lead us to a substitute formation, that is to say, a new set of beliefs comes to take the place of cultural indoctrinations. The basic indoctrinated belief is that we are truth-telling beings and that the truth can be known. Might we end our lives in the belief that truth cannot be realized, after we finish internalizing *The Confidence Man?*

I think that Melville's vision is less ironic and more tragic than that of many of his European contemporaries, though it may be that Melville's vision is simply of necessity American. For the consequence of understanding Melville's way of presenting contradiction and repression is admitting the process of thought that Freud referred to as primary-process thinking. It is the process in which the rules of logic, of empirical observation and induction, of constancy of character, and of moral probity are deformed, even suspended, as the instinctual demands overwhelm logical thought. Melville gives us a straightforward warning of the price we pay for our inability to become fully conscious of our traditional beliefs.

Thus the reader is led to recognize—though conscious affirmation may be too much to expect—the indeterminacy of traditional texts and teachings that we *believed* for so long were a sustaining force in our cultural tradition. If we accept Melville's argument as it slowly emerges from the depths of the masking in *The Confidence Man*, then we do affirm the book itself. But we affirm it with all the cultural contradictions we sustain when we read through the Apocrypha, set as it is in the central place between two bastions of truth. So out of paradox is born a simple, terrible belief, a belief that tramples upon the religious and philosophical beliefs of the past. That modern belief is this: that basic human contradictions are unresolvable. Tender sensibilities can never tolerate such a conclusion. The thrashing machine of truth has indeed separated out truths from falsehoods with a vengeance comparable to the wrath of God at the Last Judgment—a vengeance as destructive to security in the tradition of revealed truth as that threatened by the preacher who cried out that he brought Good News.

AFTERWORD

The deepest paradox within *The Confidence Man* is generated by Mocmohoc's statement, "Treachery? pale face! 'Twas they [the White man] who broke their covenant first, in coming all together; they that broke it first, in trusting Mocmohoc."

Melville's centering of this story suggest an interpretation that elevates the paradox of covenant into a theory of books and the reading of books, of the peculiar relationship between author and reader. Readers who establish a covenant with the author expose themselves to the perfidy and treachery of Mocmohoc; they deserve and shall be the object of the author's unrestrained aggression. For they expect to live in comfort with the book, while in deepest truth the book subverts their intention at every step. To make a covenant is to break the deepest relationship between author and reader, exactly the relationship proclaimed throughout *The Confidence Man*, "No Trust!" That must forever be the stance of the reader; when the reader yields to comfort and belief, the text will kill. Indeed, the letter killeth. And the conclusion of the tale, in which "the waning light expired," suggests a subversion of the psalm's reassurance, "Thy word is a lamp unto my feet, and a light unto my path." Whoever bestows such power upon the text will fall into darkness. The "light" of the story is to be found in understanding that no covenant is possible between writer and reader, just as none can be forged between Mocmohoc and the White man. The Indian *is* the artist.

I understand that such uses of "is" can be offensive, as when Freud says in his essay "The Theme of The Three Caskets" that "Cordelia is death." The psychoanalytic "is" constitutes a modern use of "is" in the history of the many uses of that verb. Philosophers have explored the "is" of logical identity, the "is" of inclusion, the "is" of causality; and the development of nineteenth-century idealism extended that exploration into the hermeneutic "is" of which the psychoanalytic constitutes one mode. We know that Freud's shorthand phrase "Cordelia is death" presupposes the whole of psychoanalytic theory of interpretation. Freud does not mean to identify Cordelia with death in an easy logical or causal sense, but demands of us that we reread the drama from a psychoanalytic, interpretative viewpoint. Freud expects a sophisticated response to his shorthand sentence. In like way, when I say the Indian in Melville's story "is" the writer, I presuppose a whole theory of interpretation as an underpinning for the claim.

The parable is intended to refer in several directions, one of which I have already explained in the main discussion of this chapter. But there is a second direction that I must point out as I just have done in the identification of Indian and author. To extend trust to another is to break a covenant; that would seem to be contradictory, for covenants are expressions of and establishments of trust. The whole book has said to us, on one level, "Have no trust"; on the next level, "To have trust is to be treacherously dealt with," therefore, beware; and on the final level, the only way to truth is through "No Trust." This suggests that the skepticism generated by the warning "No Trust" is on a deeper level a way to overcome the skepticism of the wary passenger on the ship Fidèle.

The implication for us who read is now plain: let the reader have no trust in the author, just as the White man ought to have no trust in Mocmohoc. To have trust is to break the deepest covenant, that is, the covenant of total skepticism as to all claims put forward by the book, for in seeing through the claims one opens up the possibility of discovering the truth. In this way the reader can never be betrayed by the text. For the tragedy of creativity is that it must betray those it attracts, seduces, charms in its riveting plots. Yet within the book is truth, hidden, secret, to be discovered in exactly extending *no trust* to the book. The white man cannot assume Mocmohoc's values, unless the white man becomes as treacherous as Mocmohoc; and that way is achieved in breaking the basic covenant of trust. It implies, then, denying the texts of the past to which we look for truth, especially the Bible.

Why is it that the Indian appears in the tragic themes of so many American writers? I mention, to set alongside of Melville, Thoreau, *Walden; The Maine Woods*, and Whitman, "The Sleepers," 1855 edition, *Leaves of Grass* (to be discussed in the Epilogue). Indians, like artists, possess the secrets of access to sources of power and natural creativity; they draw sustenance from hidden sources in nature. Both native woods-dwellers and the writer hear whisperings about them that they can interpret and project. In both cases, mere receivers of the word must take care not to understand the deliverances literally. Thus no covenant of belief is to be forged between reader and writer; rather, the only covenant is the covenant of no covenant. That is the deepest paradox of *The Confidence Man*.

Epilogue

Tragic Skepticism and Redemption of the Body

Settling a savage land, opening a New World, formed the American character in its discomfort: how could one make coherent the inherited mythic past of Greece and Rome and Jerusalem with the mythic present of primitive peoples who evinced an imagination and ferocity as great as any in ancient story? One way to establish separation and individuality was to kill off the savages; another was to weave them into the European plot to make one continuous story. That, in effect, is the great synthesis achieved by painters and writers in the New World. But such a synthesis is as inviting to heresy as any sectarian deviation, and we have seen, in *The Confidence Man*, the attack on artistic, religious, and political traditions that was generated in the New World. Within the European-American continuity there was an obvious opening for disagreement, for the heretical, for puzzling riddles and shocking comparisons; the previous chapter had the task of demonstrating their presence and their meaning in American cultural life.

In his harshly realistic appraisal of American culture, Henry Adams did not hide the internal conflicts that threatened the creative continuity between European and American culture: "European travellers who passed through America noticed that everywhere, in the White House at Washington and in log-cabins beyond the Alleghenies, except for a few Federalists, every American, from Jefferson and Gallatin down to the poorest squatter, seemed to nourish an idea that he was doing what he could to overthrow the tyranny which the past had fastened on the human mind." Then, drawing on the interpretations that saw the American struggle to be free of Europe as simple vulgarity, Adams quotes these lines of Tom Moore to illustrate how American cultural life appeared to Europeans:

145

Take Christians, Mohawks, democrats and all,
From the rude wigwam to the Congress hall—
From man the savage, whether slaved or free,
To man the civilized, less tame than he:
'T is one dull chaos, one unfertile strife
Betwixt half-polished and half-barbarous life;
Where every ill the ancient world can brew
Is mixed with every grossness of the new;
Where all corrupts, though little can entice,
And nothing's known of luxury but vice.

Adams concludes by putting the questions that both American intellectual leaders and European critics posed as they watched the New World unfold: "Could it transmute its social power into the higher forms of thought? Could it provide for the moral and intellectual needs of mankind? . . . Could it give new life to religion and art?"[1]

That last question still troubles us, especially in our contemporary efforts to come to grips with "reality." For our nation continues to relish religious revival and fundamentalist orthodoxy; we sustain a fantasy life that interposes the products of imagination between self and world. Living as we do today, more and more in images and stories, we have obscured the line that separates fantasy from reality, internal psychological entertainments from external natural events. But was it not always thus? We speculate that people in far-off times lived in the world of the epic; distant cultures organize their world perspectives according to *internal* principles. The line between fantasy and reality has always been obscured; history is as much a projection of the internal psychological world as a recording of the external natural world. We are condemned to a peculiar subjectivity, the subjectivity of the conscious being whose thought is both conscious and unconscious, whose modes of organizing ideas are governed by both primary-process and secondary-process principles of organization.

We reject—and resent—such a description of ourselves, preferring to believe we are rational, objective, and constant in the way we view the world. But at the same time we prize our dreams, fantasies, flights

1. Henry Adams, *The History of the United States of America, During the Administrations of Jefferson and Madison,* abridged and ed. Ernest Samuels (Chicago: University of Chicago Press, 1967), 121–27.

of bizarrerie; only we want them to be discounted when the final description of ourselves is drawn up. So we create an unconscious distinction between "narrative realizations of fiction" and "narrative derealizations of history." Fictions come to be *real*; history comes to be *unreal*. We see the first process in the "history" created by Kleist in *Michael Kohlhaas*; we see the second process in Henry Adams's effort to convey to us the world of the early republic. We have come to treat much of history as "derealized" and "depersonalized," to awkwardly translate Freud's term *Entfremdungsgefühl*. And we have come more and more to entertain states of belief towards our fantasy life as if it had independent reality. Narrative fiction draws us to its capacity to realize the past, as Kleist has done in *Michael Kohlhaas*. Yet side by side with the narrative fiction is the evidence of a history that has lost its hold on us. Our younger generations are moving into "derealized" history and "realized" fiction. For many who cannot find sustenance in religious belief, the museum, with its accumulation of cultural objects, has become the world. The museum, in that cultural function, becomes the transitional object, relating the person to the sense of something "other," however that other is created in the internal world of the museum-goer. The power of art to realize itself, to become "reality," is based upon the delight narrative realizations provide. We would far rather live in story than in the "factual," whatever that may be taken to be. In that way of working, images and stories establish themselves as internal reality, *real for us*, replacements for the anxiety generated by the external, whose ever-present threat of annihilation is one of the sources of art.

To ask if the New World could "give new life to religion and art" proposes a task of millennial proportions, for only occasionally, if ever, in the history of the West has such a renovation been accomplished. To think the question at all requires a courageous, and probably slightly fantastic, view of oneself. A new foundation must be laid for the task at hand, but where is the material to support a new cultural start to come from? My return to tragedy in its classical and modern forms is a deeply personal contribution towards answering the question. My experience has been bathed in the overt optimism and covert pessimism of the American tragic vision. Despite the importations of Old World traditions, the duality of old and new remains.

Might we allow the *native* voice of the New World to be heard: "native" in two senses, that of the truly indigenous dweller, the American Indian, as then called, and the native-born American whose life and art grow out of the native scene, without childhood recollections of another tradition? Of course, the truly American voice, that of the native dweller whose whole future was destroyed by the coming of the Europeans, has little opportunity to be heard. Special amplification is required; that is found by listening very carefully to poets such as Walt Whitman and Herman Melville, native in the second sense but sensitive to native voices in the first sense.

There is a special condition surrounding the telling of stories where the need is to achieve renovation, a new start. Poets dedicated to the American renovation are attempting to lift a repression generated by Old World endowments, particularly by its vision of a redemption in the life to come. If Christian promises of resurrection are to be seriously entertained, they must be rigorously examined and dramatically revised, for they deny the body. And the representational experiences of the tragic, as we have seen, bring the body forward into the harsh light of center stage.

"Resurrection" has meaning not only in theology, but also in the deepest fantasies we unconsciously entertain and express in tragic plots. Endowing the body with eternal life—raising the body to immortal permanence—is one of the fundamental purposes of tragic poetry. In the New World, the inherited avenues to that realization were all to be reshaped in the conditions of an American wilderness: Christian eschatology, classical and Elizabethan tragedy, and the creation of cultural objects through the arts stood in need of New World renovation. A dearth of inherited objects when the self enters the savage world lays a charge upon the self: create the cultural home, for the body as well as for the mind, in a basically inhospitable place.

"There is actually no place in this village for a work of *fine* art, if any had come down to us, to stand, for our lives, our houses and streets furnish no proper pedestal for it. There is not a nail to hang a picture on, nor a shelf to receive the bust of a hero or a saint."[2] So wrote Henry

2. Henry David Thoreau, "Economy," in *Walden* (New York: W. W. Norton and Co., 1966), 25–26.

David Thoreau in *Walden*, a manifesto of sorts proclaiming the way to live in the New World. After little more than a century, the conditions of cultural life in the New World not only rival but far surpass the Old World in sheer massive accumulation. Today, in the village where Thoreau grew up, the monuments to the arts are supported by infusions of money; objects receive greater care than do people. And the objects themselves represent every culture in the long history of human production. While Thoreau struggled to sustain an interest in the *Gita* and the *Iliad*, today the schoolchild has seen more art and heard more stories than Thoreau could have garnered in his lifetime.

His legacy to us was and is the manifesto he wrote, perhaps the first document of modernity produced in the New World. By that I mean simply that Thoreau's *Walden* laid out a system of the beautiful and the sublime for the New World, derived from eighteenth-century Enlightenment models, but tailored to his own and his community's needs. That the crude lives shaped by a raw land endured tragic moments he saw and recorded in his narrative—so aware of his fellow Americans' immaturities—but he could not, for himself, accept tragedy in the living of a fully self-conscious life such as the one he gallantly pursued. In the collection of tragedies I have studied here, Thoreau's manifesto represents the beginning of an American consciousness, tragic in its hidden depths, but attempting to overcome tragedy in its call for spiritual rebirth. *Walden*, then, is a mournful voice in a cultural wilderness. To us it expresses a tragic awareness; to itself it expressed the hope for a future American Enlightenment.

Culture, Thoreau insisted, if it is to be authentic, must be an *expression* from within, not an *imposition* from without. New England, he saw, had failed, except in small and relatively trivial instances, to express itself. In contrast to other cultures that had achieved expression from within, New England had suffered the imposition of alien cultures upon itself. So we can understand Thoreau's admiration for the *Gita* and the *Iliad*, both "naive" works in Schiller's sense, as contrasted with the "sentimental" that surrounded the thinker from Concord.

There were, of course, a few naive indigenous expressions, but they had an idiosyncratic presence. "What of architectural beauty I now see," Thoreau wrote, "I know has gradually grown from within outward, out of the necessities of the indweller, who is the only builder,—

out of some unconscious truthfulness, and nobleness, without ever a thought for the appearance; and whatever additional beauty of this kind is destined to be produced will be preceded by a like unconscious beauty of life."[3]

We read Thoreau with a slight condescension; he speaks in the voice of the crank; he lived with a tentative respect for the American consciousness, all the time harboring a longing for ancient heroic cultures that seemed faded beyond anything the New World could revive. How confusedly changed the conditions from his time to ours. We inherited his longings and ambivalences, but we are overwhelmed by a century's importations from all the cultures of the world and by the fragmentations of power and inequalities that flourished in America as it grew up. Thus we feel ourselves the inheritors of several cultural endowments—from the Old World of Europe, from the New World of America, and finally from the totality of world cultures whose presence now challenges us. It is not a question of finding a nail to hang a picture on, it is a question of finding a place for ourselves in the vast collections of objects we house, preserve, and adore. That cultural condition, which contrasts so markedly with Thoreau's, has created special problems for us today; yet we continue to pose Thoreau's central question, the deepest concern of the American effort to begin again: how do we grow up in culture; how do we in the New World discover and establish the authentic expression of self?

Thoreau did not live to see the representative expressions from within that enriched the New World in the later years of the nineteenth century: the poems of Walt Whitman, recognized as authentically American in his lifetime; and the poems of Emily Dickinson, unrecognized till long after her death. Their writings constitute a large part of our *philosophic* thought, however much it hides in unfamiliar forms. American letters expressed its philosophic thought in poetry, the novel, the private notebook, and the public lecture that became the essay, as in the case of Ralph Waldo Emerson. Philosophic speculation did not diminish in its transatlantic translation; rather, its generic modes of expression shifted, and the objects through which tragedy expressed itself masked themselves in a purposively American optimism.

3. *Ibid.*, 31.

But beneath the beautiful surface there lurked sublime nihilistic power.

For the American poets, tragedy is generated by and through *philosophical* difficulties expressed in the unresolvable puzzles of consciousness and moral conflict; but those philosophical problems are embedded in the developmental stages of childhood. Beginning again culturally drives thought to the earlier stages of growing up in culture.

I

Small, powerful books whose thought stands monumentally appear now and then in the history of poetic and philosophical thought. Walt Whitman's 1855 edition of *Leaves of Grass* is one that takes its place in a set that may appear disjunct to it, for I place it in a philosophical lineage.

In 1641 the first such book in the tradition we call "modern" appeared with the publication of Descartes's *Meditations*. The years 1751 and 1758 saw the publication of Hume's *Enquiry into Morals* and *Enquiry into the Human Understanding*. Shortly thereafter, Kant wrote his "reduced" version of the First Critique in the form he called *Prolegomena to Any Future Metaphysics* (1783). In 1785 Kant's *Metaphysic of Morals* joined the list of short revolutionary statements.

The nineteenth century tended to be far less terse; volumes on both sides of the Atlantic were fat. New World philosophy appeared in New World guises; much of it was written as sermon, essay, and poetry. Thus I see the first *Leaves of Grass* as philosophically stimulated and philosophically important, setting it in the tradition of eighteenth-century slimness. It has the courage to confront deep problems of reality, action, identity, and aesthetic form; it demonstrates the American belief that modes of *poetic* insight can be philosophically revolutionary. And Whitman achieved that, though often with issues that traditional philosophy shunned.

Tragedy hides in the first intimations of consciousness, in beginnings, in childhood—even, perhaps, in infancy. The poet recollects origins; the philosopher stands in midlife, mature, adult. The philosopher anticipates tragedy in endings; the final cause is the terror of a recognition: "This destruction was inevitable." But tragedy is rooted in the past; it comes as a fulfillment, a completion. That is one of its powers when put in the context of early experience. Beginnings, however, are often obscure, hidden, alluded to but not represented. We know that the hero has a beginning—often in an unfortunate birth; we know that great conflicts such as the Trojan War have mysterious, instinctual origins, even though by the time we "enter" the scene the rationalizations have all been established. Since we receive aesthetic effects from endings, we tend to scant beginnings. But the poet recognizes the wholeness of the action and always gives the source. The way the headwaters come out of the ground has a variety of representations. For our day it more often than not takes the form of childhood; so it did for the poet Whitman. New World tragedy sought new forms; plots coincided with life's everyday histories. Tragedy lies not in the ending, but in seeing the beginning and recognizing its tragic potentialities.

Emphasis upon beginnings characterizes psychoanalytic thinking about the tragic and the individual life. Tragedy is discovered in life's early stages and works its way through a predictable trajectory. Psychoanalytic interpretation of tragic enactments tends to seek beginnings, to emphasize the conflicts into which we are born—the conflicts within culture and the conflicts between self and culture.

American poetic reflections in both Whitman and Dickinson catch the often-hidden origins of conflict in the first stages of consciousness. Both poets recognize the connection between guilt and death, a lifelong struggle that generates extraordinary rage and under whose sway fantasies of destruction are expressed. Excessive anger pervades the poetry of America's two greatest poets; it is a force pitted against fate and fate's tragic outcomes. But how can that be, in the New World where one has the opportunity for a new beginning? *Beginning again!* That was the expectation. Yet every people and every tradition must give an account of beginnings: where we come from, how we get started. Whether we are indigenous inhabitants or fresh immigrants, we have a story to tell ourselves about origins and their towardness.

Philosophers tell the story through theory, fiat, constitutions, axioms of political thought. Poets must tell the story in their own linguistic way, through acts of creation of a people, a newborn self. The poetic reality is not *the* world, but *my* world.

Whitman begins with the act of generation, of self and of others, for which he uses the term "celebrate."

> I celebrate myself,
> And what I assume you shall assume,
> For every atom belonging to me as good belongs to you.[4]
>
> *([Song of Myself]*, 1–3)

"Celebrate" has many meanings: to frequent, crowd, fill, publicize, glorify, resound. In the beginning is the self and the multitude. But beginnings are also private, secretive, solipsistic, the *my* beginning no one else can enter or share. It is through this privacy that tragedy enters. Childhood is the tragic beginning. Whitman expresses the source in an essentially philosophical understanding and states the recognition as a terrifying sense of doubt. He is more dubious than the extreme skeptic, for the poet is in the grip of childhood dread that there may be no external reality.

To admit that there is such a state of childhood dubiety can come only after the bravado of adult affirmation, the self-assurance that there is a necessary being in simply being the self that I am.

> I exist as I am, that is enough . . .
>
> *([Song of Myself]*, 413)

This might be construed as a reply to the Cartesian *Cogito;* but that interpretation is probably unjustified as an attribution of conscious intent. The thought appears again, this time as a conscious answer to the *Cogito*, in Whitman's close dependent and follower, Wallace Stevens:

> I have not but I am and as I am, I am
>
> *(Notes Toward a Supreme Fiction*, 2.8)

It is not thinking that establishes the world for the American poet; the totality of the self *is* the world. Yet the New World beginning was infected by a skepticism seeking a belief. As we have already seen in the foregoing chapter, there is in the American psychological landscape a justified fear of the lie and of misrepresentation of the self. Paradoxes of language and of mask bedevil the New World, which call forth an-

---

4. All Whitman references are to the 1855 edition of *Leaves of Grass.*

gelic affirmations that it is *enough* to be as one is. For as one is—that precisely is what others challenge. And to their casting doubt upon one's solid presence and the world that that presence encloses, Whitman replies in defiance:

> Shall I postpone my acceptation and realization and scream at my
> eyes,
> That they turn from gazing down the road,
> And forthwith cipher and show me to a cent,
> Exactly the contents of one, and exactly the contents of two, and
> which is ahead?

([Song of Myself], 54–57)

To "scream at my eyes" expresses the rage of inherited doubt, the doubt that the poet is able to confront only at a stage in his writing when he has assured us that the outcome will be self-affirmation and self-substantiation. But that has been bluff, a stance of the Confidence Man, whose character was forged in the inability to escape pessimism as the Old World skepticism crossed to the New World. In the New World, only the face of optimism was to be shown; and Whitman is successful for some two-thirds of *Leaves of Grass* in showing that face. But then the mask falls off as the poet recollects childhood. Skepticism comes close to annihilating everything the poet has built around his adult life. Childhood, the beginning, reveals the tragic fate.

Philosophy has traditionally accepted and worked through the so-called problem of knowledge, but rarely considers a developmental perspective relevant to mature inquiry. Since the modern preoccupation has been with understanding the natural order, the model of knowledge is derived from the natural sciences. That rather pitilessly excludes infants and children! What sorts of external "reality" do they confront, and what sorts of objects do they need to understand? Whitman's poem that was in later editions of *Leaves of Grass* entitled "There Was a Child Went Forth" expresses the pain, anxiety, and inner fear of a total nihilism, to which the child can respond only with denial of any meaningful world. This is not the Cartesian doubt, which moves inexorably to affirmation, but the childhood familial conflict with the parents, upon whom the child depends for the establishment of any reality at all. The poem studies the external world—the objects—of childhood.

"Beginning" therefore takes on a dual reference, to history and to the self. America challenges both; the poet accepts the challenge, but only to show that to begin in history we must examine closely the only true beginning, that of private consciousness in its earliest stages. From that the deepest tragedy unfolds, the tragedy of finding and of loss.

New World poetic awareness discovered the locus of tragedy in the process of the everyday, of life lived from birth to death. There are no Fates spinning the thread and cutting it; there are no curses laid down upon a family, to be worked out through generations of bloodletting; rather, there is the common reality of everyman simply having parents, family, objects of perception, and the trial of life-passage.

The poem "There Was a Child Went Forth," quoted in its entirety here (see Appendix), is a rumination upon tragic beginnings. It is in the first stages of our awareness that we encounter the tragedy of human existence: there the deepest inevitable and unresolvable conflicts rage, and then the child experiences helplessness in the face of overwhelming force. Not fate, not time through which we all must "come to dust," but rather childhood's subversion of happiness in the family is the tragic theme the American poet sets out for us.

The poem reveals the condition under which the inevitable internalization of objects establishes a tragic action, for the process is drenched in affect:

> . . . with wonder or pity or love or dread, that object he
> became . . .

(2)

The source of the affect is revealed in the middle of the poem when the child's relationship to the parents becomes the shaping force of his character: "wholesome," "clean," and "mild" apply to the mother; "mean, angered, unjust" and "crafty lure" apply to the father (15–17). Both are received with "affection that will not be gainsayed," which in turn either endows objects with their degree of persuasive reality, or thrusts objects into anxious doubt as to their permanence:

> The sense of what is real . . . the thought if after all it should
> prove unreal,
> The doubts of daytime and the doubts of nighttime . . . the
> curious whether and how,

Whether that which appears so is so . . . Or is it all flashes and
specks?

(19–21)

Skeptical doubts are born not of logic and argument, but of childhood
experience within the family, whose reality counts for more than all
the natural cosmic events outside of the self.

The poem establishes a terrible truth, a truth more destructive to
childhood than it is even in later life: that love itself, that which we say
transcends and is impervious to the ruin of time, even love is transient
and can be destroyed, or, perhaps worse, can be false and other than it
appears. Whitman has the strength and the honesty to dig to the root
of experience, the source of all later elaborations, of later belief, and of
the adult's capacity to cope with objects as life's end approaches.

This is the true beginning of new lives in the New World, and when
we understand this we cannot wear the mask of optimism, as the poet
does, for very long, since under that mask is the child's affect-shaped
countenance. The man may assert:

To me the converging objects of the universe perpetually flow,
All are written to me, and I must get what
the writing means.

([*Leaves of Grass*], 404–5)

But the child has seen that it may be "all flashes and specks."

New World experience was able to perceive a necessary reversal in
the order of tragic actions inherited from the Old World tradition. Now
tragic plots move in a counter direction, counter to the process of life
lived in external time; life is understood if it is seen under the re-
organization that moves events "backwards," from adult consciousness
to first childhood awareness. But that way lies impotence; the poet,
Whitman insists, is the creator of the world, the great inseminator: out
of his "seminal wet" are cast "landscapes projected masculine, full-siz-
ed and golden" ([*Leaves of Grass*], 646). How can it be that out of
terrifying skepticism the child emerges as the poet who *creates* the
only reality human beings can know?

Whitman's answer came to him in a burst of energetic reconstruc-
tion that provided the answer to the question, "How can I be *at home*
when the familial has provided at best a divided home? How can I at last

feel a universal oneness when I suspected that the only 'reality' I perceived was all 'flashes and specks?' " In the first *Leaves of Grass*, one utterance unifies inner and outer experience for the unnerved child, and in that process discovers a poetic unity for the entire poem. That sequence later came to be called "The Sleepers" (see Appendix).

To master the tragedy into which each one of us is born, Whitman reaches back into the Old World vision that was preserved in Virgil's *Aeneid*, Book 6.

> The newborn emerging from gates and the dying emerging from
> gates,
> The night pervades and enfolds them.
>
> (10–11)

Virgil's dream-gates of horn and of ivory are metaphorically transformed into portals for the newborn and the dying. Whitman warns us that we will be introduced to dreams of a calm, refreshing consolation, as well as to dreams of nightmare-inducing anxiety. Just as Aeneas encounters the woman (Dido, his lover) and the man (Anchises, his father) by whom his life has been shaped, so the sleeper of "The Sleepers" meets the dominant male and female figures of his life. The father is represented by Washington, the mother by his mother as remembered through a tale of childhood betrayal.

So much can be read in the poem, but its mode of representation eludes us until we grasp its reliance upon primary-process thinking. Unlike Virgil's poem, which addresses both the gods and the ancestors, "The Sleepers" addresses dreaming itself as a meaningful disorder whose grammar and syntax we must discover. Part of that latent order lying beneath manifest disorder is to be discovered in sequence. Linguistic and developmental sequences inter-inanimate one another in the section beginning with the fantasy so private that Whitman censored it in later printings of the poem:

> O hotcheeked and blushing! O foolish hectic!
> O for pity's sake, no one must see me now! . . . my clothes were
> stolen while I was abed,
> Now I am thrust forth, where shall I run?
> Pier that I saw dimly last night when I looked from the windows,
> Pier out from the main, let me catch myself with you and
> stay . . . I will not chafe you;

I feel ashamed to go naked about the world,
And am curious to know where my feet stand . . . and what is
  this flooding me, childhood or manhood . . . and the hunger
  that crosses the bridge between.

The cloth laps a first sweet eating and drinking,
Laps life-swelling yolks . . . laps ear of rose-corn, milky and just
  ripened:
The white teeth stay, and the boss-tooth advances in darkness,
And liquor is spilled on lips and bosoms by touching glasses, and
  the best liquor afterward.

I descend my western course . . . my sinews are flaccid,
Perfume and youth course through me, and I am their wake.

It is my face yellow and wrinkled instead of the old woman's,
I sit low in a strawbottom chair and carefully darn my grandson's
  stockings.

(60–70 [removed in later editions]; 71–74)

Descent into the "underworld" now takes on a psychological meaning, for the poem has delved into the unconscious processes of imagistic thinking, offering a sequence of images whose inner connections we must discern. Here is the order of poetic "argument" stated in its simplest imagistic terms:

1. "My truant lover has come and it is dark."
2. Fantasy of stolen clothes
3. Pier and nakedness
4. Fantasy of yolks, corn, teeth, liquor
5. Flaccid sinews
6. Become the old woman darning stockings
7. Gigantic swimmer: midlife vigor
8. Washington (father) bids farewell to the troops
9. Mother's story about the squaw
10. Lucifer: "my tap is death"

This sequence of dream episodes weaves itself into the plot of a tragedy that at first seems to lack beginning, middle, and end, because of the violently fragmented central events of the poem. Yet the poem asserts coherence, harmony, and reconstituted wholeness at the end. We can think of that as a catharsis if we wish, but I find readily imposed coherence a way of overcoming or interpreting optimistically the descent into the underworld. Like Aeneas, the poet in America can visit the shades and there encounters anxiety-arousing scenes but must return to bring a message of hope and vision of future progress, a vision that transforms the fears of darkness into the hopes of daylight.

I suspect that, like Aeneas, the speaker of "The Sleepers" was returned through the Ivory Gate, the gate from which false dreams issue. The implication is that the memory of the visit to Hades, just as the visit to the unconscious, must be obliterated. Otherwise, action in this world of waking cannot proceed without debilitating depression.

The going under brings the visitor from the land of the living to inevitable, ever-present tragedy; the process by which our lives are pulled together into a coherent whole—whether in dream or in mantic prophecy—reveals to us the tragedy of human existence. Both Aeneas and the speaker of "The Sleepers" have woven together fragments of life lived: infancy, childhood, adolescence, young love, adult duty, parents, and memories of ecstatic orgasmic moments—all solidify into a plot that now can be experienced with a beginning, middle, and end. According to the revelation received "underground," the story must end in tragic impotence and separation. Above ground, the poet asserts the harmony of happy conclusions and reifies it in works, cities, and poems; and tragedy is overcome in the symbolism of a return to the loving mother:

> I will duly pass the day O my mother and duly return to you.
>
> (202)

The life-giving plot of "The Sleepers" tells the story of growing up; each stage of life receives its moment, from earliest symbiosis with the mother, through childhood and youth, to the majestic farewell to the weeping father as Washington fades away into the history of the Revolution and the poet separates himself from the father. But the close dependence upon the mother and the undying love of the mother for the child, love that ought to survive all vicissitudes, are subverted by another woman, the Indian squaw who steals the mother's love. Abandoned and depressed, the child entertains the tragic denouement: the mother is killed. But in the fantasy, it is the thieving possessor of the mother who dies. The steamboat has carried away his woman; his retaliation is lethal: "My tap is death." The conflict, inevitably, has ended in tragedy. But the underworld dream-life yields to the wishes of love once again, and in a second ending, as it were, the child is reunited with the mother.

That truly is a new beginning, but it must live side by side with the old ending.

Whitman was able to imagine himself the Christ, with the power to raise bodies from the dead. But it is the poet, through his art, who performs the miracle. "Resurrection" may have emerged from poetry as a theological idea, but it was initially, and now is again, a poetic idea. Through art the body gains eternal presence, transcends space and time; while in the here and now we are coerced by space and time. It was the philosopher, Kant, who suggested that we escape space and time through the experience of the beautiful (see chapter 4). But he learned that from art itself, and we have seen the reassertion of resurrection in a nonreligious context in modern American tragedy. The search for survival midst the necessities of causality and mortality forced the poet, Walt Whitman, to recreate an Old World dream vision (entertained once by mature wanderers in midlife) in the unconscious of a child.

II

Whitman's contemporary, Emily Dickinson, sees her poetic statements as dramatically determined. She is on a stage, playing a part, donning masks, unmasking, integrating space and time of performance into the self; for if space and time can be internalized, they become *expressions* of the body. And the body is the object we wish to survive, to achieve immortality, to be resurrected. If space and time can be internalized, then survival of death is achieved. The way to a life-after is not through conventional belief; that is an anodyne explored in many of the poems, in which common (and deeply suspect) biblical preachments are subjected to doubt. The life-after, insofar as it transcends mere belief, can only be a function of *poetry*, for that is the stage upon which we work out the metaphysical possibilities realistically open to us. Poetic utterance creates little dramas out of our dreaming and our waking states.

> We dream—it is good we are dreaming—
> It would hurt us—were we awake—

But since it is playing—kill us,
And we are playing—shriek—
What harm? Men die—externally—
It is a truth—of Blood—
But we—are dying in Drama—
And Drama—is never dead—

Cautious—We jar each other—
And either—open the eyes—
Lest the Phantasm—prove the Mistake—
And the livid Surprise

Cool us to Shafts of Granite—
With just an Age—and Name—
And perhaps a phrase in Egyptian—
It's prudenter—to dream—

(531)[5]

The poem sums up and stands as a coda to the tragic choices we have seen in the development of modern tragedy. We can say to ourselves, "Thank God it's only a dream!" and then deny the dream ("livid surprise"); thus we wake, and when we wake we become a sepulcher with an inscription, which means we die once and finally and are turned into stone—death as monument.

Or we can stay in the horrible dream, which is the prudent choice— that is, to be an actor-character who is playing death all the time: "we are playing—shriek—". We are perpetually in play of a deadly kind, but it goes on without waking *if* we can tolerate the play(ing). To die in the drama of life is to die perpetually; to die in reality is to be turned into a stone monument, and that is lifelessness, though it warns generations to come.

In drama one is always dying, yet never dead; in life we *really* die, and while that is a certain relief, it is an ending. The implication, then, is that the better way is to remain in the representation of art, where we play shriek and go on dreaming.

But we in the drama of death try to wake one another up because we fear the Phantasm, i.e., we fear that the drama we are dreaming is a

5. All quotations are from *The Complete Poems of Emily Dickinson*, ed. Thomas H. Johnson (Boston: Little, Brown and Co., 1960).

mistake. But it is the *truth* of life, and *that* we find hard to accept. We tell ourselves this is a "livid surprise." The term "livid" has two meanings: bluish, bruised, and discolored; and ashen or pallid. It merges the thoughts of mistake and ghost. But we are truly done for if we wake, for then we are turned to stone, as if we had looked upon the Gorgon, with nothing of us to survive but an Egyptian-like shaft of granite. It is better (prudenter) to dream on in a perpetual shriek of death.

We never die if we live life as art, but that is to say we are always dying in art as life. But to be always in play-that-is-death is to transcend space and time by internalizing them; this is another way of saying that which Kant explored as the only human means to escape the determinism of the Newtonian and the denial of space-time in the moral life: that is, the power of art to make space-time conform to *our* needs as feeling beings. In art, we live outside of the spatiotemporal realm, in the sense that space-time is *within* us; and though it is dream, it is eternity—in the only human sense that can be given to that term. Within the spatiotemporal realm we are spatiotemporal shafts of granite; we are not in representational action any longer, but simply symbols to be deciphered by generations who come after us.

This complex working through of the ways art and life are related takes as its basic metaphor the tragic drama. The drama that most fully reflects these thoughts—perhaps the drama underlying the thought of this poem—is Shakespeare's *Macbeth*, for there sleep has been "killed"; sleep, "great Nature's second course, / Chief nourisher in life's feast," has been murdered by Macbeth. He has attempted to overcome space and time and has failed, through making a direct assault on the day-to-day human existence *within* space and time. In that assault he has killed the one psychological retreat granted to us in our peculiar metabolism, the without-space-and-time realm of sleep. But that overcoming is realized by the artist through his *art*, in the drama itself, and we who watch enter into dramatic "immortality."

It is the author's task to bring us to the reality of the drama within which the reflections on reality and finality can be entertained. Dickinson's poem as philosophical drama poses the question that we, the audience, must confront: do we stay in the dream, or do we rush away from the supposed Phantom of art, only to be turned to stone as we step out of dream into reality?

One force—almost instinctual—that drives us to seek escape is the radical condition of our birth, which, again, is a mirror of art, as art is a mirror of being born and dying shriek! Here is the poetic argument that puts forth our human riddle—the riddle we live our lives seeking to resolve:

> I am afraid to own a Body—
> I am afraid to own a Soul—
> Profound—precarious Property—
> Possession, not optional—
>
> Double Estate—entailed at pleasure
> Upon an unsuspecting Heir—
> Duke in a moment of Deathlessness
> And God, for a Frontier.

(1090)

"Double Estate—entailed at pleasure" refers to the endowment bestowed upon each human being: body and soul. "At pleasure" has two senses: at the pleasure of (according to the wish of) the one who makes the endowment, the parents or God; and the means whereby the endowment is realized, the pleasure of sex. With the endowment, consequent upon the "pleasure" of will and of sex, come the Deathlessness and the Frontier or boundary conditions under which the entailment is made. Each of us is duke over the domain that extends to the Frontier that is God, the boundary that separates the human from all that lies beyond. "Duke" comes from Genesis 36:40, as Dukes descended from Esau; hence we are entailed as property of God, but also as inheritors of immortality. And we are thus endowed whether we like it or not, because the "at pleasure" is that driving sexual pleasure Yeats called "Honey of generation."

Birth conditions define the human domain in terms that fit into the limits of representation and reality as explored in poem 531. In this poem (1090), we explore the limits set upon earthly life as a "gift"—but a gift with terrifying implications. The two poems together define the transitional points in the journey of life, which we are challenged to accept or pass through: the life lived in dramatic representation and the conditions of generation that make the life in representation possible at all. We may not be able to pass through, because the boundary is impermeable; we may fail to achieve the immortality of dramatic life because of the failed use of our inheritance, through fear of "ownership."

Recognition of those points, and getting past them or through them, is the task of explorations belonging to art; but the art object comes to us as the person comes into life: body and soul entailed at pleasure. The artist in the act of generation presides over all the aspects of sexual life.

A final theme in this New World exploration of dramatic representation is stated in a poem examining the sexual stages of development that the art-life imposes upon the poet:

> Which is the best—the Moon or the Crescent?
> Neither—said the Moon—
> That is best which is not—Achieve it—
> You efface the sheen.
>
> Not of detention is Fruition—
> Shudder to attain.
> Transport's decomposition follows—
> He is Prism born.
>
> (1315)

To be "Prism born" is to come to be in the breaking up of the whiteness of light, and the breaking up of white into its constituent colors has two meanings: the physical, Newtonian meaning; and the decomposition of transport, which is the breaking up of the self following the sexual shudder—that is, orgasm. To "efface the sheen" has again several meanings: creativity takes away the sheen, the beauty of the beautiful woman (as in Middle English, e.g., "Emily the sheen" means "the beautiful, effulgent Emily"). Creation (artistic) and procreation (sexual) are dependent upon giving up the surface beauty of the self, breaking the self into colors, which leads to the new beauty of the created object. In the process of creativity it is meaningless to ask which is best, the Moon or the Crescent, because to be creative one must be in a constant process of phase development and phase maturation. Fruition, for the Moon and for the woman, necessitates the shudder, the decomposition, the breaking of the Sheen and the white light into their colors. Moon and woman, as usual, are exchangeable. When the poet is transported by the sexual shudder, decomposition follows; that is, the breaking of the self on behalf of the birth is a "decomposition." Persons *and* poems are born, out of the sexual shudder, the decomposition that recomposes self and language into the resurrected fragments, now made whole.

Mythic fantasies inhabit New World poetry: Emily Dickinson and Walt Whitman rewrote and redrew mythic scenes and characters, setting them in philosophical dramas. Their utterances, a manifesto to our ears, announce a renovation of the tradition whose earlier explorations, in Old World and in New, have been examined in the chapters of this book. To trace the fate of tragedy in modernity, I have used both philosophical and psychoanalytic modes of inquiry, methods to map the landscape in which three roads meet: the political-historical, the psychosexual, and the unconscious. Tragedy reveals the universality and inevitability of conflicts generated at historical junctions, but never "solves" the problems represented in dramatic poetry. Rather, tragedy presents itself in and through cultural objects; their fate is decided by communities that call upon—or ignore—their presence. It is for each generation to decide the value and the wisdom of the tragic understanding.

For my generation, the use of tragic wisdom has been directed on the one side to the interpretation of political conflicts and on the other to confined private conflicts within the person. By bringing together philosophical and psychoanalytic methods of inquiry, this extended domain is encompassed; the two complement one another in their capacities to address different, yet interrelated, experiences. The chapters making up this inquiry attempt to exhibit ways in which the two traditions—philosophical and psychoanalytic—work with each other in the interpretation of cultural objects, the enactments of tragedy. I hope the confluence has enabled me to discover and to uncover hidden presences of tragedy where perhaps tragedy was not perceived before. Tragedy, for its part, contributes to our understanding of philosophy and psychoanalysis: by regarding tragedy from philosophical-psychoanalytic viewpoints and then turning around to regard philosophy and psychoanalysis through the prism of tragedy, a new kind of cultural event takes place. We today use terms such as "interdisciplinary" or "multidisciplinary" to describe the method and its outcome, but that is simply a classification of this book. In itself the book represents a stage of the consciousness of modernity, a stage that will not be fully understood until it passes into the history of culture; then we shall ourselves be, perhaps, immodest subjects of future study. That in itself is a tragic destiny.

Appendix

Walt Whitman, *Leaves of Grass* (Edition of 1855)

[*There Was a Child Went Forth*]

There was a child went forth every day,
And the first object he looked upon and received with wonder or
    pity or love or dread, that object he became,
And that object became part of him for the day or a certain part of
    the day . . . . or for many years or stretching cycles of years.

The early lilacs became part of this child,
And grass, and white and red morningglories, and white and red
    clover, and the song of the phoebe-bird,   5
And the March-born lambs, and the sow's pink-faint litter, and the
    mare's foal, and the cow's calf, and the noisy brood of the
    barnyard or by the mire of the pondside . . and the fish
    suspending themselves so curiously below there . . and the
    beautiful curious liquid . . and the water-plants with their
    graceful flat heads . . all became part of him.

And the field-sprouts of April and May became part of him . . . .
    wintergrain sprouts, and those of the light-yellow corn, and of
    the esculent roots of the garden,
And the appletrees covered with blossoms, and the fruit afterward
    . . . . and woodberries . . and the commonest weeds by the
    road;
And the old drunkard staggering home from the outhouse of the
    tavern whence he had lately risen,
And the schoolmistress that passed on her way to the school . . and
    the friendly boys that passed . . and the quarrelsome boys
    . . and the tidy and freshcheeked girls . . and the barefoot
    negro boy and girl,   10
And all the changes of city and country wherever he went.

His own parents . . he that had propelled the fatherstuff at night,

and fathered him . . and she that conceived him in her womb
and birthed him . . . . they gave this child more of themselves
than that,
They gave him afterward every day . . . . they and of them became
part of him.

The mother at home quietly placing the dishes on the suppertable,
The mother with mild words . . . . clean her cap and gown . . . . a
wholesome odor falling off her person and clothes as she walks
by: 15
The father, strong, selfsufficient, manly, mean, angered, unjust,
The blow, the quick loud word, the tight bargain, the crafty lure,
The family usages, the language, the company, the furniture . . . .
the yearning and swelling heart,
Affection that will not be gainsayed . . . . The sense of what is real
. . . . the thought if after all it should prove unreal,
The doubts of daytime and the doubts of nighttime . . . the curious
whether and how,   20
Whether that which appears so is so . . . . Or is it all flashes and
specks?
Men and women crowding fast in the streets . . if they are not
flashes and specks what are they?
The street themselves, and the facades of houses . . . . the goods in
the windows,
Vehicles . . teams . . the tiered wharves, and the huge crossing at
the ferries;
The village on the highland seen from afar at sunset . . . . the river
between,   25
Shadows . . aureola and mist . . light falling on roofs and gables
of white or brown, three miles off,
The schooner near by sleepily dropping down the tide . . the little
boat slacktowed astern,
The hurrying tumbling waves and quickbroken crests and slapping;
The strata of colored clouds . . . . the long bar of maroontint away
solitary by itself . . . . the spread of purity it lies motionless in,
The horizon's edge, the flying seacrow, the fragrance of saltmarsh
and shoremud;   30
These became part of that child who went forth every day, and who
now goes and will always go forth every day,
And these become of him or her that peruses them now.

[The Sleepers]

[I]

I wander all night in my vision,
Stepping with light feet . . . . swiftly and noiselessly stepping and
    stopping,
Bending with open eyes over the shut eyes of sleepers;
Wandering and confused . . . . lost to myself . . . . ill-assorted . . . .
    contradictory,
Pausing and gazing and bending and stopping.   5

How solemn they look there, stretched and still;
How quiet they breathe, the little children in their cradles.

The wretched features of ennuyees, the white features of corpses, the
    livid faces of drunkards, the sick-gray faces of onanists,
The gashed bodies on battlefields, the insane in their strong-doored
    rooms, the sacred idiots,
The newborn emerging from gates and the dying emerging from
    gates,   10
The night pervades them and enfolds them.

The married couple sleep calmly in their bed, he with his palm on
    the hip of the wife, and she with her palm on the hip of the
    husband,
The sisters sleep lovingly side by side in their bed,
The men sleep lovingly side by side in theirs,
And the mother sleeps with her little child carefully wrapped.   15

The blind sleep, and the deaf and dumb sleep,
The prisoner sleeps well in the prison . . . . the runaway son sleeps,
The murderer that is to be hung next day . . . . how does he sleep?
And the murdered person . . . . how does he sleep?

The female that loves unrequited sleeps,   20
And the male that loves unrequited sleeps;
The head of the moneymaker that plotted all days sleeps,
And the enraged and treacherous dispositions sleep.

I stand with drooping eyes by the worstsuffering and restless,
I pass my hands soothingly to and fro a few inches from them;   25
The restless sink in their beds . . . . they fitfully sleep.

The earth recedes from me into the night,
I saw that it was beautiful . . . . and I see that what is not the earth
    is beautiful.

I go from bedside to bedside . . . . I sleep close with the other
    sleepers, each in turn;
I dream in my dream all the dreams of the other dreamers,   30
And I become the other dreamers.

I am a dance . . . . Play up there! the fit is whirling me fast.

I am the everlaughing . . . . it is new moon and twilight,
I see the hiding of douceurs . . . . I see nimble ghosts whichever
    way I look,
Cache and cache again deep in the ground and sea, and where it is
    neither ground or sea.   35

Well do they do their jobs, those journeymen divine,
Only from me can they hide nothing and would not if they could;
I reckon I am their boss, and they make me a pet besides,
And surround me, and lead me and run ahead when I walk,
And life their cunning covers and signify me with stretched arms, and
    resume the way;   40
Onward we move, a gay gang of blackguards with mirthshouting
    music and wildflapping pennants of joy.

I am the actor and the actress . . . . the voter . . the politician,
The emigrant and the exile . . the criminal that stood in the box,
he who has been famous, and he who shall be famous after today,
The stammerer . . . . the wellformed person . . the wasted or feeble
    person.   45
I am she who adorned herself and folded her hair expectantly,
My truant lover has come and it is dark.

Double yourself and receive me darkness,
Receive me and my lover too . . . . he will not let me go without
    him.

I roll myself upon you as upon a bed . . . . I resign myself to the
    dusk.   50

He whom I call answers me and takes the place of my lover,
He rises with me silently from the bed.

Darkness you are gentler than my lover . . . . his flesh was sweaty
    and panting,
I feel the hot moisture yet that he left me.

My hands are spread forth . . I pass them in all directions,   55
I would sound up the shadowy shore to which you are journeying.

Be careful, darkness . . . . already, what was it touched me?
I thought my lover had gone . . . . else darkness and he are one,
I hear the heart-beat . . . . I follow . . I fade away.

O hotcheeked and blushing! O foolish hectic!   60
O for pity's sake, no one must see me now! . . . . my clothes were
    stolen while I was abed,
Now I am thrust forth, where shall I run?

Pier that I saw dimly last night when I looked from the windows,
Pier out from the main, let me catch myself with you and stay I
    will not chafe you;
I feel ashamed to go naked about the world,   65
And am curious to know where my feet stand . . . . and what is this
    flooding me, childhood or manhood . . . . and the hunger that
    crosses the bridge between.

The cloth laps a first sweet eating and drinking,
Laps life-swelling yolks . . . . laps ear of rose-corn, milky and just
    ripened:
The white teeth stay, and the boss-tooth advances in darkness,
And liquor is spilled on lips and bosoms by touching glasses, and the
    best liquor afterward.   70

[2]
I descend my western course . . . . my sinews are flaccid,
Perfume and youth course through me, and I am their wake.

It is my face yellow and wrinkled instead of the old woman's
I sit low in a strawbottom chair and carefully darn my grandson's
    stockings.

It is I too . . . . the sleepless widow looking out on the winter
    midnight,   75
I see the sparkles of starshine on the icy and pallid earth.

A shroud I see—and I am the shroud . . . . I wrap a body and lie in
    the coffin;
It is dark here underground . . . . it is not evil or pain here . . . . it is
    blank here, for reasons.

It seems to me that everything in the light and air ought to be
    happy;
Whoever is not in his coffin and the dark grave, let him know he
    has enough.   80

[3]
I see a beautiful gigantic swimmer swimming naked through the
    eddies of the sea,
His brown hair lies close and even to his head . . . . he strikes out
    with courageous arms . . . . he urges himself with his legs.

I see his white body . . . . I see his undaunted eyes;
I hate the swift-running eddies that would dash him headforemost
    on the rocks.

What are you doing you ruffianly red-trickled waves?   85
Will you kill the courageous giant? Will you kill him in the prime
    of his middle age?

Steady and long he struggles;
He is baffled and banged and bruised . . . . he holds out while his
    strength holds out,
The slapping eddies are spotted with his blood . . . . they bear him
    away . . . . they roll him and swing him and turn him:
His beautiful body is borne in the circling eddies . . . . it is continually
    bruised on rocks,   90
Swiftly and out of sight is borne the brave corpse.

[4]
I turn but do not extricate myself;
Confused . . . . a pastreading . . . . another, but with darkness yet.

The beach is cut by the razory ice-wind . . . . the wreck-guns
    sounds,
The tempest lulls and the moon comes floundering through the
    drifts.   95

I look where the ship helplessly heads end on . . . . I hear the burst

as she strikes . . I hear the howls of dismay . . . . they grow
fainter and fainter.

I cannot aid with my wringing fingers;
I can but rush to the surf and let it drench me and freeze upon me.

I search with the crowd . . . . not one of the company is washed to
us alive;
In the morning I help pick up the dead and lay them in rows in a
barn.   100

[5]
Now of the old war-days . . the defeat at Brooklyn;
Washington stands inside the lines . . he stands on the entrenched
hills amid a crowd of officers,
His face is cold and damp . . . . he cannot repress the weeping
drops . . . . he lifts the glass perpetually to his eyes . . . . the
color is blanched from his cheeks,
He sees the slaughter of the southern braves confided to him by their
parents.

The same at last and at last when peace is declared,   105
He stands in the room of the old tavern . . . . the wellbeloved
soldiers all pass through.

The officers speechless and slow draw near in their turns,
The chief encircles their necks with his arm and kisses them on the
cheek,
He kisses lightly the wet cheeks one after another . . . . he shakes
hands and bids goodbye to the army.

[6]
Now I tell what my mother told me today as we sat at dinner
together,   110
Of when she was a nearly grown girl living home with her parents on
the old homestead.

A red squaw came one breakfastime to the old homestead,
On her back she carried a bundle of rushes for rushbottoming chairs;
Her hair straight shiny coarse black and profuse halfenveloped her
face,
Her step was free and elastic . . . . her voice sounded exquisitely as
she spoke.   115

173

My mother looked in delight and amazement at the stranger,
She looked at the beauty of her tallborne face and full and pliant
    limbs,
The more she looked upon her she loved her,
Never before had she seen such wonderful beauty and purity;
She made her sit on a bench by the jamb of the fireplace . . . . she
    cooked food for her,   120
She had no work to give her but she gave her remembrance and
    fondness.

The red squaw staid all the forenoon, and toward the middle of the
    afternoon she went away;
O my mother was loth to have her go away,
All the week she thought of her . . . . she watched for her many a
    month,
She remembered her many a winter and many a summer,   125
But the red squaw never came nor was heard of there again.

Now Lucifer was not dead . . . . or if he was I am his sorrowful
    terrible heir;
I have been wronged . . . . I am oppressed . . . . I hate him that
    oppresses me,
I will either destroy him, or he shall release me.

Damn him! how he does defile me,   130
How he informs against my brother and sister and takes pay for
    their blood,
How he laughs when I look down the bend after the steamboat that
    carries away my woman.

Now the vast dusk bulk that is the whale's bulk . . . . it seems mine,
Warily, sportsman! though I lie so sleepy and sluggish, my tap is
    death. . . .
        [8]

The sleepers are very beautiful as they lie unclothed,
They flow hand in hand over the whole earth from east to west as
    they lie unclothed;   180
The Asiatic and African are hand in hand . . the European and
    American are hand in hand,
Learned and unlearned are hand in hand . . and male and female
    are hand in hand;
The bare arm of the girl crosses the bare breast of her lover . . . .

they press close without lust . . . . his lips press her neck,
The father holds his grown or ungrown son in his arms with
     measureless love . . . . and the son holds the father in his arms
     with measureless love,
The white hair of the mother shines on the white wrist of the
     daughter,   185
The breath of the boy goes with the breath of the man . . . . friend
     is inarmed by friend,
The scholar kisses the teacher and the teacher kisses the scholar . . . .
     the wronged is made right,
The call of the slave is one with the master's call . . and the master
     salutes the slave,
The felon steps forth from the prison . . . . the insane becomes sane
     . . . . the suffering of sick persons is relieved,
The sweatings and fevers stop . . the throat that was unsound is
     sound . . the lungs of the consumptive are resumed . . the
     poor distressed head is free,   190
The joints of the rheumatic move as smoothly as ever, and smoother
     than ever,
Stiflings and passages open . . . . the paralysed become supple,
The swelled and convulsed and congested awake to themselves in
     condition,
They pass the invigoration of the night and the chemistry of the
     night and awake.

I too pass from the night;   195
I stay awhile away O night, but I return to you again and love you;
Why should I be afraid to trust myself to you?
I am not afraid . . . . I have been well brought forward by you;
I love the rich running day, but I do not desert her in whom I lay
     so long:
I know not how I came of you, and I know not where I go with you
     . . . . but I know I came well and shall go well.   200

I will stop only a time with the night . . . . and rise betimes.

I will duly pass the day O my mother and duly return to you;
Not you will yield forth the dawn again more surely than you will
     yield forth me again,
Not the womb yields the babe in its time more surely than I shall
     be yielded from you in my time.

175

Index

Index